Spain

Spain

Text by Emma Stanford
Updated by Norman Renouf
Photography: Chris Coe & Conor Caffrey;
except pages 120: Bill Wassman;
122, 128: Jon Davison;
and page 104: Claude Huber
Cover Photo: Conor Caffrey
Layout by Dial House Publishing Services Ltd
Cartography by Raffaele DeGennaro
Managing Editor: Tony Halliday

Second Edition 2002

NO part of this book may be reproduced, stored in a retrieval system or transmitted in any form or means electronic, mechanical, photocopying, recording or otherwise, without prior written permission from Apa Publications. Brief text quotations with use of photographs are exempted for book review purposes only.

CONTACTING THE EDITORS
Every effort has been made to provide accurate information in this publication, but changes are inevitable. The publisher cannot be responsible for any resulting loss, inconvenience or injury. We would appreciate it if readers would call our attention to any errors or outdated information by contacting Berlitz Publishing, PO Box 7910, London SE1 1WE, England. Fax: (44) 20 7403 0290;
e-mail: berlitz@apaguide.demon.co.uk

CONTENTS

● A ☛ in the text denotes a highly recommended sight

Spain

SPAIN AND ITS PEOPLE

Spain is located in the far southwest of Europe and comprises the largest part of the Iberian Peninsula (with Portugal claiming a narrow strip hugging most of the western coastline). The Balearic islands of Ibiza, Mallorca and Minorca, in the western Mediterranean, also belong to Spain, as do the subtropical Canary Islands, off the west coast of Africa.

Magnificent in Its History

Starting with the Phoenicians' founding of Cádiz in 1,100 B.C., Spain was colonized over a period of some 2,500 years by such diverse cultures as the Carthaginians, Romans, Vandals, Visigoths and the Moors, all of whom contributed something to the character of the country. It was not until the Catholic Monarchs, Ferdinand and Isabella, drove the last remaining Moors from their capital in Granada in 1492 that Spain became a united country. At the same time, the previously harmonious relationship between Catholics and people of Jewish and Moorish origin was broken by the Spanish Inquisition, which saw the latter two groups persecuted and expelled from the country. The same year saw the event that started Spain's golden era — the first modern European voyage to America led to Spain becoming fabulously rich with wealth from her Southern American colonies. These treasures, however, were soon squandered in pointless wars and Spain retreated, introspectively, behind the formidable barrier of the great Pyrenees mountain range.

It was a desperately poor Spain that re-emerged onto the international stage in 1936, torn asunder in a violent, murderous Civil War between the left-leaning Republicans — assisted by the famed International Brigades — and the right-wing Nationalists led by General Franco — and helped by German and Italian military might. After his victory in 1939, Franco instituted a harsh dictatorship that ended only with his death in 1975. Uniquely though, and not over-looking the negative effects of his era, he planned for a democratic constitutional monarchy to succeed him — successfully as it has turned out. Since then four general elections have seen the government controlled first by centrists, then by socialists and now by the Partido Popular, a right-of-center party. During the last two decades, more and more power has devolved to the 17 autonomous regions.

Magnificent in Its Scenery

Monumental mountain ranges, such as the Pyrenees and Sierra Nevada, as well as numerous lesser-known ranges, are spread throughout Spain's mainland. And, not to be outdone, the Canary Island of Tenerife boasts Mount Teide — the highest mountain in the country. Along Spain's Atlantic and Mediterranean coasts — and, of course, on the islands — one finds most every conceivable type of beach environment. Inland are powerful rivers; arid plateaus; wide plains and even, in Almería and on the island of Fuerteventura, a real desert environment. What is more, while Spain is (at 504,880 sq km/194,885 sq miles) the third largest country in Europe, after Russia and France, it has a proportionately small popu-lation. Consequently, and unusually in Europe, vast areas of the country remain wild, rugged and under-populated.

Magnificent in Its People

Spain's varied terrain and the assimilation of so many diverse cultures have shaped the character of her peoples. And it is, in reality, peoples in the plural — not people in the singular. Most of Spain's 17 autonomous regions are fiercely independent — both in their thinking and in their relative free-dom from interference by central government, a combination that has given rise to passionate "regional nationalism." The Catalans, Basques and Valencianos, among others, are delighting in their new-found independence. This is reflected most obviously for visitors by the use of local languages rather than Castilian Spanish. In fact, only around 60 per cent of Spaniards use Castilian as their natural language.

Even though the regions differ widely in custom and character, they generally share a very "Spanish" lifestyle. This includes a love of children, devotion to family and friends, and an open and inclusive social life that includes partaking of much fine food and wine. Generally, Spaniards are a garrulous, happy and contented people who place much importance in politeness, both with each other and strangers.

Magnificent in Its Variety

Spain is such a large country and there is so much to see and do, practicalities dictate that there is no way you can expect to see it all in one vacation. It is best to select an itinerary for a first-time visit that takes in the most important cities of historical interest that appeal to your particular interests. And, your

Ancient windmills and Moorish-era castles enliven the magnificent landscapes of Spain.

The Gaudí-designed Casa Battló is typical of Barcelona's architectural bravura and style.

choices will be many. The variety of scenery and attractions in Spain promises that there will be something of interest here to the novice or the seasoned traveler, and everyone in between.

Madrid is the Spanish capital and transportation hub, located at the geographical heart of the country and is the most obvious place to start. Not only is it of importance in its own right, but it can also be used as a base to visit a host of fascinating nearby cities and places of interest.

Barcelona, world famous for its architecture and style, should be high on everyone's list of priorities. In fact, if anything, it has more individual attractions than Madrid, and it is surrounded by places of great interest. **Andalucía**, a name that is evocative of passionate emotion, is a must. But as the region is so large, visitors should concentrate, first, on the cities of **Sevilla**, **Córdoba** and **Granada**. Each of these has so much to see that it is difficult to choose between them — so try to get to them all.

Many millions of people visit Spain each year with the aim of simply relaxing on a beach, and for this they have numerous options. The world-renowned **Costas** stretch from the Costa Brava at the eastern end of the Pyrenees all the way round past Gibraltar to the Costa de la Luz and the border with Portugal. Less well known is the **Costa Verde** (Green Coast), which is quite different in most all aspects from The Costas, and stretches along the northern coast passing through Cantabria, Asturias and Galicia on its way from the Basque Country to the Portuguese border. Don't forget, either, the **Balearic Islands** off Spain's eastern Mediterranean coast, with resorts that range from the rowdy to the refined. Visitors from the northern hemisphere in search of serious winter sunshine and swimming need look no further than the volcanic **Canary Islands**. Just off the coast of North Africa, these seven islands are as different from each other as it is possible to be.

Spain also has scores of places that far fewer visitors get to see. **The Basque Country**, an entity unto itself, is graced by the elegant town of **San Sebastián** and by the stylish city of **Bilbao**, home to the new Guggenheim Museum. Ancient **Castilla y León** has the fine old Castilian cities of **Burgos**, **León**, **Palencia**, **Salamanca**, **Soria**, **Valladolid** and **Zamora**. **Navarra** is famous all over the world for the bull-running that forms part of the San Fermín Festival in **Pamplona**. **La Rioja**, famous for its wines, and the old kingdom of **Aragón** stretches from the high Pyrenees down to its capital **Zaragoza** and on to **Teruel**.

Bilbao's striking Guggenheim Museum has won worldwide plaudits for the Basque capital.

Spain

Between Madrid and Andalucía are two of the least-visited regions of Spain: **Castilla-La Mancha**, to the east and south, is well known for its wines; and the isolated city of **Cuenca** is famous for its Casas Colgadas (Hanging Houses). **Extremadura** has always been remote, but that didn't stop the Romans from making **Mérida** one of its most important towns. **Cáceres**, also founded by the Romans, is important these days for the collection of 16th-century palaces and other structures in its "Monumental Zone."

Slabs of caramel and ochre against a deep blue sky turn Cuenca's famous Hanging Houses into abstract art.

A BRIEF HISTORY

Spain's history is as rugged and colorful as the land itself. It is a tale of Roman and Moorish domination and a glorious Golden Age; of empires and colonies conquered and defeated; of brave knights and foolish kings; and of a bloody and destructive Civil War that saw Spain cut off from the international community for some three decades of the 20th century. Yet, almost unbelievably, some thirty years after the death of Franco, the rehabilitation of Spain appears to be complete.

Early History

The earliest inhabitants of the Iberian Peninsula were Paleolithic people who probably arrived via a land bridge linking Europe and Africa between Gibraltar and Morocco. As the Ice Age gripped Europe, the first Iberians put on bearskin coats, stoked up their fires, and fed off deer, bison, and wild horses — just like those depicted on the walls and ceilings of caves discovered in Cantabria, near Altamira, which date back at least 15,000 years.

During the Bronze Age, Celtic migrants settled in northern and central Spain, while the south and east were inhabited by various Iberian tribes of North African origin. The Iberians had their own written language, sophisticated industry, and tools, and they created fine works of art, such as the stone sculpture of a female deity, known as La Dama de Elche (The Lady of Elche), a star attraction at Madrid's Archaeological Museum. The Celts and the Iberians interacted where their territories over-lapped and developed a distinct Celtiberian culture. The Celtiberians soon gained fame as soldiers and it is said that they invented the two-edged warrior's sword (later to become standard equipment in the Roman army, and to be used against their inventors).

Before this, Phoenicians, sailing from bases in North Africa, founded several colonies in southern Spain. The first of these, founded in about 1100 B.C., was Gadir (present-day Cádiz). Carthage, which was itself a Phoenician colony, established an empire of its own that spread as far north into Spain as Barcelona and the island of Mallorca. The Carthaginians exploited Spain's silver and lead mines and drafted the country's young, able-bodied males into their army. Barcelona was the base from which Carthaginian forces under Hannibal set out to defeat Rome in the third century B.C., nearly succeeding in their objective before being defeated by the Romans in the Second Punic War. The defeat of the Carthaginians left the way open for Rome to take control of the peninsula, though it took nearly 200 years to subjugate the stubbornly resistant Celtiberians.

Spain under the Caesars

Second only to the homeland itself, Spain was to become the most important part of the Roman Empire. All over the country the stamp of Roman civilization

Mérida's Roman theater is still used for plays during the summer festival.

Historical Landmarks

3,000 B.C.	Bronze-Age Celts in the north, Iberians the south.
1,100 B.C.	Phoenicians found Gadir (Cádiz).
third cen. B.C.	Carthaginians conquer much of Spain.
first cen. B.C.	Romans complete their conquest of Spain.
first cen. A.D.	Christianity introduced.
fourth cen.	Decline of the Roman Empire.
sixth cen.	Visigoths make Toledo their capital.
711	Moors take Andalucía and control most of Spain.
722	Christian Reconquest begins at Covadonga.
758	Córdoba becomes the Moorish capital.
1474	Ferdinand of Aragon marries Isabella of Castile.
1478	Inauguration of the Inquisition.
1492	Jewish and Arab expulsion. Columbus's voyage.
1516	Charles I inherits the Spanish throne.
1556–1598	Philip II rules from Madrid.
1588	Defeat of the Spanish Armada.
1618–1648	The Thirty Years' War.
1701–1714	The War of Spanish Succession. Philip V wins the crown.
1804–1814	The War of Independence.
1833–1876	Internal strife: the Carlist Wars.
1898	The Spanish-American War: end of empire.
1914–1918	Spain is neutral in World War I.
1923–1930	Primo de Rivera's dictatorship supported by king.
1931	Anti-monarchist election victory; king into exile.
1936	Left-wing government elected; start of Civil War.
1939	Republicans defeated; Franco in power.
1955	Spain joins the United Nations.
1975	Franco dies; King Juan Carlos accedes.
1977	Political parties legalized.
1978	October 31, new democratic constitution ratified. Spain joins NATO.
1986	Spain joins the EU.
1992	Barcelona Olympics; Seville hosts Expo '92.
1996	Election won by the right wing Partido Popular.
2000	The Partido Popular increased its majority at the General Election with José María Aznar remaining as Prime Minister.

remains in walls and roadways, villas, monuments, and vineyards. Three living Spanish languages are descended from Latin: Gallego (Galician), Castilian, and Catalan. Roman law forms the foundation of the Spanish legal system, and Spain gave birth to Roman emperors as memorable as Trajan and Hadrian, as well as the writers Seneca and Martial.

The Romans divided the peninsula into two: Hispaniae Ulterior and Hispaniae Citerior ("Farther" and "Nearer" respectively). When it was later carved into three provinces, the capital cities were established at what are now Mérida (Extremadura), Córdoba (Andalucía), and Tarragona (Catalonia). Christianity came to Spain early in the Roman period. The word may have been carried by St. Paul himself (he is said to have preached both in Aragón and at Tarragona).

The Visigoths

Overstretched and increasingly corrupt, Rome watched its far-flung colonies disintegrate, and Germanic tribes, some with a deserved reputation for barbarism, hastened into the vacuum. The Vandals had little to contribute to Spanish culture. However, the Gaulish Visigoths from France did bring a certain constructive influence. Former allies of Rome, they ruled from Toledo, where they displayed their intricate arts and built opulent churches.

The 300-year regime of the Visigoths never achieved any measure of national unity, and eventually foundered on the thorny question of succession. The commendably democratic principle of elective monarchy fostered a web of intrigue and assassination as contenders attempted to secure the crown. These, as well as other problems, were often blamed on the handiest scapegoat: the industrious and successful Jews. They had fared well under the Romans and early Visigoths, but at the start of the seventh century, all non-Christians were forced either to convert to Christianity or face exile.

Enter the Moors

During A.D. 711, an expeditionary force of around 12,000 Berber troops from North Africa sailed across the Straits of Gibraltar and poured ashore into Spain. Their expertly planned invasion was led by General Tariq ibn Ziyad (the name Gibraltar is a corruption of Gibel Tariq — Tariq's Rock). His ambition was to spread the influence of Islam.

Within just three years, the Moors or *moriscos* (as North African Muslims are usually called in Spanish history) had reached the Pyrenees. Due in part to the Visigoths' military disorganization, the Moors' initial success was also assisted

The distinctive style of this cloister in San Juan de Duero reflects the fusion of Moorish and Christian elements.

El Cid's prowess as a soldier is immortalised in epic poetry.

by ordinary citizens attracted by promises of lower taxes and by serfs offered the chance of freedom. Spanish Jews welcomed the Moors as liberators because, initially at least, the occupation forces stipulated religious tolerance. However, conversion to Islam was later forcefully encouraged, and many Christians chose to embrace the Muslim creed.

The most tangible relics of this time are now among Spain's greatest tourist attractions: the exquisite Moorish palaces and mosques of Córdoba, Granada, and Seville. Thanks to the irrigation techniques imported from North Africa, crops like rice, cotton, and sugar were planted, and lush orchards of almonds, pomegranates, oranges, and peaches thrived. Other Moorish innovations made possible the production of paper and glass, and the art of medieval Moorish artisans is preserved in today's best Spanish craft buys — ceramics, tooled leather, and intricate silverwork.

The Christians Strike Back

The Moorish juggernaut that trundled north from Gibraltar in 711 met no serious resistance. It was eleven years before the fragmented defenders of Christian Spain won their first battle. Exiled to the northern territory of Asturias, the

Visigothic nobles, led by Pelayo, joined with local mountain folk to strike the first blow in the long-drawn-out Reconquest of Spain. Further Christian victories would be a very long time in coming, but Pelayo's success at the Battle of Covadonga (the village is now a shrine) sparked off the desire to defeat the Moors and gave heart to a struggle that was to simmer for centuries.

In the middle of the eighth century, the Christians of Asturias, under King Alfonso I, took advantage of a rebellion by Berber troops to occupy neighboring Galicia. Here, at Santiago de Compostela, the alleged discovery of the tomb of the apostle St. James (Santiago) was to make Compostela the religious focus for Spanish Christians and a rallying point for knightly defenders of the Christian faith throughout Europe. More breathing space from

---

El Cid

The legend of El Cid, Spain's national folk hero, is recounted in the epic poem *El cantar de mío Cid*. Born Rodrigo Díaz de Vivar in around 1040 near Burgos, he was a highly successful soldier of fortune. Vivar at first fought for the kings of Castile in the battle against the Moors. When Sancho II died in mysterious circumstances, Vivar humiliated his successor, Alfonso VI, by forcing him to swear publicly that he had nothing to do with Sancho's death. Exiled for his impudence, Vivar joined the Moors, from whom he received his honorary title, El Cid (Arabic for "Lord"). El Cid's greatest victory was in 1094, when he led a Christian-Moorish army to take Valencia, where he died in 1099. Encouraged by his death, a Moorish army regrouped to take the city. El Cid's body was propped on his horse and ridden before the defending army, which routed the attackers.

Moorish pressure was won in what we now know as Catalonia. Charlemagne, King of the Franks, captured Catalonia's capital, Barcelona, and established a buffer zone here between Islamic Spain and France. Spanish Christians then seized the advantage and expanded south and west into the area between Catalonia and Asturias, which soon had so many frontier castles that it became known as Castile.

The Reconquest see-sawed on for hundreds of years, as each side gained and lost territorial advantage under a succession of leaders. Over the centuries, squabbles among the Moors resulted in alliances of convenience with the Christians, and the intermingling of the two cultures was commonplace. Christians who thrived in the Moorish regions were known as Mozarabes, and their Moorish counterparts — Muslim inhabitants of Christian enclaves — were known as Mudéjars. These two names are now attached to the two most important art styles of this period, which are a blend of both Christian and Moorish elements.

Much suffering accompanied the Reconquest of Spain.

Early in the tenth century, the Asturian capital was transferred approximately 120 km (75 miles) south from Oviedo to León, a symbolic step deep into former "infidel" territory. However the Muslims were far from on the run. United under the dictator al-Mansur ("the victorious"), they reclaimed León, Barcelona, and Burgos and, in a severe blow to Christian morale, sacked the town of Santiago de Compostela. The death of the charismatic al-Mansur in 1002 revived Christian hopes. In 1010, they succeeded in recapturing al-Mansur's headquarters of Córdoba, and the city of Toledo fell in 1085.

The fall of Toledo sent out shock waves to Moorish rulers elsewhere in Spain and they called for help from the Almoravids, a North African confederation of Muslim Berber tribes based in Marrakesh. Known for their military prowess, they halted the Reconquest, but in the 12th century sent for further reinforcements from the Almohad fundamentalists, who stepped up the persecution of Jews and Mozarabes. The turning point of the Reconquest is held to be the Battle of Las Navas de Tolosa in 1212. In its wake, the Christian forces regained most of Spain south to Andalucía, the point where the final Moorish stronghold at Granada was recaptured in 1492.

A Singular Nation

Up until the 15th century, the various regional kingdoms of Spain remained resolutely independent. There were some sporadic moves towards unity, which usually involved strategic marriage contracts, and it was one such royal marriage that united the shrewd Ferdinand of Aragón and strongly religious and patriotic Isabella of Castile. Under the reign of the Catholic Monarchs (as Pope Alexander VI entitled them), a single Spain was

A legacy of the Reconquest era, the stout walls of Ávila are perfectly preserved with no less than 90 towers.

created, comprising most of the nation we know today, though the component parts of the newly united kingdom retained their individuality and their institutions.

Aiming to further unite the country, Ferdinand and Isabella inaugurated the Inquisition in 1478. Initially intended to safeguard religious orthodoxy under Isabella's influential confessor, the fanatical Tomás de Torquemada, it became a byword for the persecution of Jews, Muslims, and, later, Protestants. Several thousand suspected heretics were horribly tortured and many were publicly burned at *autos-da-fé* (show trials). In 1492, Torquemada convinced Ferdinand and Isabella to expel the surviving unconverted Jews — perhaps 200,000 in all, including some of the country's best-educated and most productive citizens.

The year 1492 was a momentous one for Spanish history. Not only did it witness the expulsion of the Moors and the Jews, but also Europe's discovery of the New World by

Genoese explorer **Cristobal Colón** (Christopher Columbus). Sponsored by Queen Isabella (who, according to legend, pawned her own jewels to raise the money), the expedition and subsequent annexation of the New World territories laid the foundations for Spain's Golden Age.

The Hapsburgs

While Ferdinand and Isabella were Spain personified, their grandson and heir to the throne, Charles I, born in Flanders in 1500, could barely compose a sentence in Spanish. Through his father, Philip, Duke of Burgundy, he inherited extensive possessions in the Low Countries; he was appointed Holy Roman Emperor (Charles V) in 1519. An unpopular king, Charles alienated his Spanish subjects by appointing Flemish and Burgundian supporters in key posts such as Archbishop of Toledo and regent during his frequent absences. Charles's expansionist foreign policies consolidated Burgundy and the Netherlands as Spanish provinces. He also annexed Milan and Naples and drew Spain into a series of costly European wars funded from the seemingly bottomless pit of Spain's New World bounty.

In 1556, overwhelmed by his responsibilities, Charles abdicated in favor of his son, Philip II. Born and educated in Spain, the new king gave top jobs to Castilians and proclaimed Madrid his capital, thereby converting an unimpressive town of 15,000 into the powerhouse of the greatest empire of the age. As literature and the arts flourished, Philip worked endlessly to administer his over-extended territories. He captured Portugal, and shared in the glory following the destruction of the Turkish fleet at Lepanto (1571). However, the destruction of the Spanish fleet in the disastrous Armada episode (1588) and the spiraling costs of maintaining the empire eventually robbed Philip of his health and severely depleted the Spanish treasury. He died in devout seclusion at El Escorial, the palace-monastery in the hills northwest of Madrid.

Though Spain was still the dominant force in Europe at Philip's death, the Golden Age and empire were on the wane. Philip III delegated his responsibilities to his favorites, involved Spain in the Thirty Years' War between the Catholic and the Protestant parts of Europe, and expelled the remaining *moriscos,* many of them farmers, thereby precipitating an agricultural crisis.

The final century of the Hapsburg era saw a gradual, then a rapid, decline in Spanish fortunes. Ironically, in contrast to the severe loss of territorial possessions and despite the ravages of war, pestilence, and famine, the works of Velázquez, Zurbarán, Murillo, and Ribera bear witness to the achievements of Spanish artists of the age.

The last of the Spanish Hapsburgs, Charles II, died heirless in 1700. His crown went to the Duke of Anjou, grandson of Louis XIV of France, who claimed the title as Philip V of Spain. Archduke Charles of Austria (another Hapsburg) contested the claim, which sparked the War of the Spanish Succession, ended by the Treaty of Utrecht in 1713.

Bourbons on the Throne

Philip V eventually secured the throne, but his diminishing empire was now shorn of Belgium, Luxembourg, Milan, Sicily, and Sardinia. To add insult to injury, Britain snatched strategic Gibraltar. The most successful Spanish king of the 18th century, Charles III, recruited capable administrators, disbanded the Inquisition, invigorated the economy, and paved the streets of Madrid. But Spain came increasingly under the power of France during the Bourbon period.

Spain's Bourbon rulers transformed a former Hapsburg hunting ground to create Madrid's elegant Retiro Park.

After the defeat of the Franco-Spanish fleet by the British at the Battle of Trafalgar in 1805, Charles IV had to abdicate. Napoleon tried to appoint his brother Joseph as José I, but the Spanish rose against the French, resulting in the Peninsula War (which Spaniards call the War of Independence). In 1814, with the help of British troops led by the Duke of Wellington, the French were finally ousted. While this was going on, several of Spain's most valuable American colonies took advantage of her preoccupation to win their independence.

With Ferdinand VII on the throne, a Bourbon king once again ruled Spain, but the country failed miserably to prosper. Political infighting, a repressive monarchy, and anti-clerical revolts led to the domestic Carlist Wars. The century ended with another disaster as Cuba, Puerto Rico, and the Philippines were lost in the Spanish-American War.

The Spanish Civil War

Spain escaped the horrors of World War I, watching the carnage from a position of neutrality. Alfonso XIII backed the dictatorship of General Miguel Primo de Rivera (1923-1930), but went into exile (never to return) after anti-royalist forces won a landslide victory in the 1931 elections. The new Republic was riven with bitter ideological conflicts, particularly between the Left and Right. A left-wing victory in the 1936 elections and the assassination of the Monarchist leader, Calvo Sotelo, ignited nationalist and conservative fears of a Marxist revolution. Monarchists, clergy, and the right-wing Falange organization united behind the Movimiento Nacional, led by the war hero General Francisco Franco. Meanwhile, a motley band of liberals, communists, socialists, and anarchists cast their lot with the newly elected Spanish government.

The inevitable outcome was the Civil War: three years of horrific bloodshed and destruction which gutted towns and cities and claimed between 50,000 and 75,000 lives, as father fought son and region battled against region. Franco emerged victorious, but Spain was shattered, physically and emotionally.

The New Spain

Although he was sympathetic to the Axis powers during World War II, Franco opted for neutrality, and quietly began to rebuild Spain. The trains ran on time and the streets were safe again, but there was a heavy atmosphere of repression, and economic recovery was slow. On Franco's death in 1975, his chosen successor was Juan Carlos de Borbon, grandson of Alfonso XIII, who was crowned king of a constitutional monarchy, and has proved an able and popular king on Spain's road to democracy.

Fundamental changes in the political landscape came thick and fast in the 1970s and 1980s as the Falange was wound down, the Communist party legalized, and varying degrees of autonomy were granted to the seventeen regions. Today, as a member of the United Nations, NATO, and the EU, Spain's long separation from the world and European mainstream is over.

The last few years have seen further remarkable changes in the world view of Spain, and in the national psyche. The formerly poor relation of Europe is now economically strong, culturally vibrant, and well placed to look ahead with confidence to the new challenges of the 21st century.

Bilbao's Guggenheim Museum symbolises the new, modern and progressive Spain.

WHERE TO GO

👉 MADRID AND ENVIRONS

Settled by the Romans in the second century B.C., Madrid was occupied by the Moors in 711. Under Mohammed I, the Moors fortified the town in 865, and made it a walled city. Just over two centuries later, in 1083, Madrid was reconquered by King Alfonso VI. Fernando IV summoned the Courts of the Kingdom in 1309, the Catholic Monarchs ordered the de-fortification of the city's walls and gates in 1476 and, in 1561, Felipe II moved the court to here from Toledo, thus making Madrid the capital of a vast empire.

The early part of the next century, during the Hapsburg era, saw the very important addition of the Plaza Mayor. The House of Bourbon succeeded the Hapsburgs, and it was this dynasty that was responsible for many of the grand and attractive buildings and monuments that adorn the city today.

Among these are the Royal Palace, completed in 1764; the Alcalá gate, raised in 1778 to honor Carlos III's entry into the city as king, and the Prado Museum constructed between 1785 and 1819. During the Spanish Civil War, from November 1936 to March 1939, the city was subject to a three-year siege by the Nationalist

Depicted in tile, Madrid's symbol is a bear eating the leaves of a strawberry tree.

forces, whose eventual entry into Madrid ended hostilities.

Madrid is the largest city in Spain and, at an elevation of 655 m (2,100 ft), the highest capital in Europe. The ambiance of this hustling, bustling modern city reflects an intriguing blend of old and new. It also makes a good base for exploring several historic nearby towns. The best way to get around town is by the cheap and efficient metro system (subway).

There is much to see in Madrid and the best place to start is the bustling **Puerta del Sol** (Gate of the Sun), the hub of ten converging streets. This is liter-

Allegorical frescoes enliven the Casa de la Panadería's façade.

ally the crossroads of Spain, known as "Kilometre 0" in the country's highway system, and home to an imposing equestrian statue of Carlos III and a smaller statue depicting Madrid's coat-of-arms — a bear standing against a *madroño* (arbutus, or strawberry) tree.

A few blocks west is the **Plaza Mayor** (Main Square), a 17th-century architectural masterpiece. Its broad arcades surround a vast, traffic-free, cobbled rectangle, once used as the inner-city showground where bullfights, pageants, and even public executions took place. Today, an equestrian statue of Felipe II surveys rows of outdoor cafés and lively summer-season festivals. The plaza's two most famous houses are the **Casa de la Panadería** (Bakers Guild) which holds some of the city archives, and the **Casa de la**

Carnicería (Butchers Guild) whose façades are decorated with a series of vibrant, and even mildly erotic, paintings.

Continuing west on Calle Mayor, Plaza de la Villa juxtaposes stately 16th- and 17th-century buildings of differing styles. These include the lovely **Casa de Cisneros,** which belongs to the ornate and delicate style of architecture known as Plateresque (*platero* means silversmith), and the towering Hapsburg-era **Ayuntamiento** (City Hall).

The **Palacio Real** (Royal Palace), to the north, is set among formal gardens on a bluff overlooking the Manzanares Valley. Felipe V commissioned this imposing French-style palace on the site of the old Moorish fort, and furnished its 2,000 rooms (more than any other European palace except the Hermitage in St Petersburg) in a suitably regal fashion. As it is a working palace, the opening hours are unpredictable. Join one of the hour-long tours that visit around 50 rooms, including the overwhelmingly rococo Gasparini Room, the Ceremonial Dining Room with seating for 145 guests, and the Throne Room with its stunning Tiepolo ceiling frescoes. Other diversions to see include the Royal Armoury, the Pharmacy, and the Library.

The **Gran Vía** is Madrid's main thoroughfare. Lined with shops, hotels, restaurants, theaters, cafés, and nightclubs, it cuts a wide path west to east from Plaza de España to the busy round Plaza de la Cibeles, so named for the Cybele Fountain that is adorned with a sculpture of a Greek fertility goddess.

Art lovers are spoilt for choice in Madrid. The **Convento de las Descalzas Reales** (Royal Descalzas Monastery), located behind the El Cortes Ingles store at the Puerto del Sol, became a retreat for the Kings of Castile. Today, it is a dignified museum housing many important works of art. The **Real Academía de Bellas Artes**, also close to the Puerto del

Madrid Highlights

Museo del Prado: *Paseo del Prado; Tel. (91)420 37 68 or web site <www.mcu.es/prado>.* Housed in 18th-century neo-classical grandeur, this is one of Europe's most famous art museums and not to be missed. It displays art treasures amassed by the Spanish monarchy. Tuesday–Saturday 9am–7pm, Sunday and holidays 9am–2pm. €3.00, free on Saturday after 2pm and Sunday. (See page 32).

Palacio Real: *Calle de Bailén; Tel. (91) 542 00 59. Metro: Opera.* Principal residence of Spanish kings from Felipe V in the mid-18th century until Alfonso XIII was exiled in 1931. Monday–Saturday 9am–6pm, Sunday and holidays 9am–3pm (closed on state occasions). €6.00 for guided tour. (See page 30).

Centro de Arte Reina Sofía: *Santa Isabel 52; Tel. (91) 467 50 62. Metro: Atocha.* Modern art museum housing many Picasso masterpieces. Monday, Wednesday–Saturday 10am–9pm, Sunday 10am–2:30pm. €3.00, free after 2:30pm on Saturday and Sunday. (See page 32).

Fundación Thyssen-Bornemisza: *Paseo del Prado 8; Tel. (91) 369 01 51 or web site <www.museothyssen.org>. Metro: Banco.* Some 800 superb artworks on semi-permanent loan. Tuesday–Sunday 10am–7pm. €4.20. (See page 32).

Convento de las Descalzas Reales: *Plaza de las Descalzas; Tel. (91) 547 53 50. Metro: Callao.* This 16th-century Convent has been handsomely endowed with art treasures. Tuesday to Saturday 10:30am–12:45pm, 4pm–5:45pm and Monday in the afternoon. €4.20. (See page 30).

Real Academia de Bellas Artes: *Alcalá 13; Tel. (91) 522 00 46. Metro: Sol.* None of the crowds you get at the Prado; you can linger over the Goya paintings. Tuesday–Friday 9am–7pm, Saturday–Monday 9am–2:30pm. €2.40, free on Saturday and Sunday. (See page 30).

Museo Arqueológico: *Calle Serrano 13; Tel. (91) 577 79 12. Metro: Serrano.* An overview of Spain's cultural heritage illustrated by archaeological finds, with a replica of the Altamira cave complex in the gardens. Tuesday–Saturday 9:30am–8:30pm; Sunday 9am– 2pm. €2.40.

Sol, has a fine collection of paintings by Goya. The fabulous and world-famous **Museo del Prado** is, deservedly, Spain's most visited attraction. The Prado houses what is indisputably the world's greatest collection of Spanish paintings, and a particularly strong set of Italian and Flemish masterpieces. If time is short, plan ahead and decide what you want to see beforehand. Likely top-of-the-list sights are works by El Greco (1541–1614), Ribera (1591–1652), Zurbarán (1598–1664), Felipe IV's court painter Velázquez (1599–1660 (whose *Las Meninas*, or Maids of Honour, is said to be Spain's favorite painting), Murillo (1617–1682), and magnificent Goya (1746–1828). Of the Dutch and Flemish masters, be sure not to miss works by Hieronymous Bosch, called "El Bosco" here, and Rubens. The Italian Old Masters include works by Raphael, Titian, and Tintoretto. Nearby, a Prado annex, the **Casón del Buen Retiro**, houses the museum's treasure trove of 19th-century Spanish art, while directly opposite the main museum, the **Fundación Thyssen-Bornemisza** spans 700 years of artistic endeavor from the Italian primitives to Pop Art. Just a short distance to the south the **Centro de Arte Reina Sofía** boasts important collections of modern art and many masterpieces by Picasso — including the monumental *Guernica* that was inspired by the horrible Civil War bombing of a Basque village.

If the sightseeing and the bustle get too much, the enormous **Parque del Retiro** behind the Prado is a favorite spot for *madrileños* out for a stroll. Originally a 17th-century Hapsburg hunting ground, it offers 121 hectares (300 acres) of leafy avenues, flower beds, and park benches, including a rose garden, boating lake, and Sunday morning sideshows. There are also cafés, exhibitions in the Palacio de Cristal and Palacio de Velázquez, and a botanical garden founded by Carlos III in 1781.

AROUND MADRID

Toledo

Located on a strategic hill protected by the encircling River Tagus, Toledo is a fascinating and historical city. Conquered by the Romans in 193 B.C., it was the Visigoths, who had overrun the Vandals, who made Toledo their political and religious capital in the fifth century A.D. After the Moors invaded Spain, in A.D. 711, the city was incorporated into the Córdoba Emirate. After the Emirate disintegrated in 1012, it became the capital of an independent kingdom. In 1085 King Alfonso VI of León re-conquered Toledo and made it his capital, a status it retained until 1561 when Felipe II, grandson of the Holy Roman Emperor Carlos (Charles) V, moved the capital to Madrid. This marked the beginning of the decline of the importance of Toledo, even though it remained the seat of the Primate of Spain.

Unquestionably the most important monument in the city is the **Catedral**. The first

Toledo's mighty Alcázar fortress was besieged as recently as the 1936 Civil War.

one on this site was built jointly by the Visigoth King Recaredo I and the first Bishop of Toledo, San Eugenio. Converted into a mosque by the Moors, it was not until 1227 that King Ferdinand III "The Saint" began construction of the present building. It wasn't finally completed until the 16th century and as it incorporates numerous architectural styles it is known as the "Museum Cathedral". The **coro** (choir) and main altar are marvels of woodcarving. Just behind the main chapel, Narciso Tomé's baroque **Transparente** is an 18th-century masterpiece and in the **Sala Capitular** (Chapter House) there is an intricate ceiling in the Mudéjar style.

A curious tradition here are the strange looking hats hanging precariously from the ceiling; if you look closer, you'll notice they are suspended over plaques which indicate tombs of primates buried below. Each of these hats belonged to the respective primate and when they fall — and it could be days or centuries later — the tomb is then removed to the vaults. Don't miss, either, the **Tesoro** (Treasury) with its religious artworks, including 18 paintings by El Greco, and Enrique de Arfe's Monstrance. Made of solid silver and gold it has over 5,600 individual parts and weighs in at a very substantial 200 kg (430 lbs).

Toledo Steel

Toledo is famous all over the world for the quality of its steel, and swords have been forged here since Roman times. According to legend, the special property of the steel is inherited from the magical water of the River Tagus. Look for **damascene** steel souvenirs. This is a craft unique to the city, which involves inlaying black steel with decorative gold, copper, and silver filigree.

The city of Toledo occupies a high rocky mound, almost surrounded by a deep gorge formed by the River Tajo.

Dominating the city is the huge **Alcázar**, a fortress destroyed and rebuilt many times since the Roman era — most recently during the Civil War. Rebuilt since then, except for a few rooms left as a reminder of a harrowing story, it now houses an Army Museum and has displays relating to the dramatic 72-day Civil War siege.

El Greco is inextricably linked with Toledo. His first commission was to paint the reredos at the **Cistercian Convent of Santo Domingo de Silos** which, founded in 1085 by King Alfonso VI, is the oldest monastery in Toledo. The original contract is actually on display and he and his family are also interned here. More famously, his *Burial of the Count of Orgaz*, a fascinating depiction of local noblemen attending the count's funeral, is on display at the church of **Santo Tomé** — also notable for its landmark Mudéjar tower. The young boy attending upon the saints is considered to be a likeness of El Greco's son, and on a handkerchief dangling from the boy's pocket he signed his name, Doménico Theotokopouli, and the date, 1583. El Greco spent the most productive years of his prolific painting career in Toledo. Just downhill from Santo Tomé, a house in which he is said to have lived has been reconstructed and now forms the **El Greco's House and Museum**. More of El Greco's work, and many other interesting things as well, can be found at the 16th-century **Hospital de Santa Cruz** (Holy Cross Hospital).

El Greco's House was originally built by Samuel Levi, a 14th-century Jewish financier, and a friend of King Peter I of Castile. He constructed **La Sinagoga del Tránsito** next to his home and Muslim artists adorned the walls with intricate filigrees and Hebrew inscriptions from the Psalms. These days the synagogue is a national monument and also home to the **Museo Sefardí** (Museum of Spanish Judaism). Not far away is the **St Mary the White Synagogue**, which resembles a mosque and has a simplicity of style that enhances its ambiance.

Just down the street is a fine church with royal connections. Ferdinand and Isabella, whose emblems of the different realms combined by their marriage sit either side of the altar, built **San Juan de los Reyes** (St John of the Kings) to celebrate victory at the Battle of Toro in 1476. In a mix of Mudéjar, Gothic, and Renaissance styles, it was also meant to be the Catholic Monarchs' last resting place. That was before they became enchanted with Granada, which was captured in 1492. There is also a superb double-height cloister with elaborate stone carvings.

There are numerous other churches, museums and monuments in Toledo but one, in particular, should not be missed. The **El Cristo de la Luz** (Christ of the Light) dates from the 10th century, and functioned as a mosque until the

Reconquest. It is the only building in the city from that era to have survived in its original condition.

Ávila

Located 112 km (70 miles) northwest of Madrid, at an altitude of 1,128 m (3,700 ft) above sea level, Ávila is the highest city in Spain. With origins in the Celto-Iberian era, it was Christianized in the first century A.D., and after nearly three centuries of Moorish rule was reconquered by King Alfonso VI in 1085. After the Reconquest the city was repopulated by

St Teresa of Ávila (1515–82) was renowned for her mystic visions and reforming zeal.

Christian knights who began work on what is unquestionably Ávila's most dominant feature: **Las Murallas** — the walls. These are an average of over 3.65 m (12 ft) high and 2.7 m (9 ft) thick. Built into their nearly 2.7-km (1⅔-mile) length are nine gateways and 90 towers. Noblemen were responsible for defending a particular section of the wall. Consequently, many elegantly fortified mansions were built near or as an integral part of the walls. Even the 12th- to 16th-century **cathedral**, combining Romanesque, Gothic, and Renaissance elements, has a **cimorro** (fortified head) built into the walls.

Ávila's spiritual influence is a legacy of St Teresa, who was beatified on March 12, 1622. She was born here in 1515 and her influence, in the shape of churches, convents and statues, is on display throughout the city. A Catholic visionary and advocate of Carmelite thought, she founded no less than seventeen convents throughout Spain and wrote prolifically. She lived for 30 years in the Convent of the Incarnación, outside the city walls, first as a novice and for the last three years as prioress.

Just outside the city walls, the **Basilica de San Vicente** — commemorating St Vincent of Zaragoza and his two sisters who were martyred in the fourth century — is noted for an extraordinary tomb topped by a bizarre oriental canopy.

Though located away from the town center, the **Monasterio de Santo Tomás** should not be missed. Dating from 1482, it has been managed by the Dominican Order and was also used frequently by the Catholic Monarchs as a summer residence. Ferdinand and Isabella's only son, Don Juan, died here at the age of 19 and his very impressive sepulcher is in the chapel. Treasures acquired by Dominican missionaries on their Far Eastern travels are exhibited here in the Oriental Art Museum.

After viewing Ávila up close, drive or take a bus across the Río Adaja to the monument called **Los Cuatro Postes** (The Four Posts). Curious in itself, it consists of four Doric columns connected by cornices, each of which is decorated with the city's coats-of-arms, with a stone cross in the center. More importantly, the hill offers a panoramic view of the whole of medieval Ávila, which is especially impressive when floodlit at night.

☛ San Lorenzo de El Escorial

At an elevation of 1,065 m (3,494 ft) in the foothills of the Sierra de Guadarrama, by the town of El Escorial, about 49 km (30 miles) northwest of Madrid you will find a building of absolutely massive proportions. Visible from many miles away, this monastery was commissioned in 1557 by Felipe (Philip) II to commemorate his victory over Henri II of France at the Battle of San Quentín, an event that took place on August 10, the Feast Day of **San Lorenzo** (Saint Lawrence). Extended over the years, it boasts 86 stairways, more than 1,200 doors, and 2,600 windows, summing up the physical and spiritual superlatives of the empire's Golden Age.

The monastery is actually a multi-faceted complex, comprised of royal living quarters, a basilica, monastery, pantheon, elaborate library, and art galleries and museum all under one roof. The **apartments of Felipe (Philip) II** are modest in comfort but rich in art, and include a fantastic triptych by Hieronymus Bosch. The **Palacio Real** (Royal Palace) has a succession of lavishly decorated rooms, notably the **Sala de las Batallas,** adorned with frescoes depicting complex battle scenes, and fine tapestries. Of the dozens of works of art collected in the great **basilica** —

Despite being one of Europe's most powerful monarchs, Felipe II lived an almost monastic life at El Escorial.

which is part **Sotocoro** (people's church), part monastic church and part royal — none attracts more admiration than Cellini's life-sized marble crucifix. Felipe II died here in 1598 and, along with the remains of almost all Spain's monarchs and their families from the 17th century onwards, is buried in the elaborately fascinating royal **pantheon**. The **library**, with its baroque ceiling adorned with a series of magnificent frescoes by Tibaldi, is particularly spectacular and contains some 40,000 rare books, plus priceless and beautiful manuscripts. The **New Museums** display masterpieces by Ribera, Tintoretto, Velázquez, and El Greco. In 1984 El Escorial was declared a World Heritage Monument by UNESCO.

Just around the mountain is another monument of magnificent proportions, albeit one of a very different type. After the Spanish Civil War, Generalíssimo Franco wanted to build a monument to commemorate those who died during the hostilities. As a site he chose the V-shaped valley called Cuelgamuros, in the Sierra de Guadarrama, known today as the **Valle de los Caidos** (Valley of the Fallen). Of the two disparate parts, the most visible — from miles around — is a huge cross standing 150 m (492 ft) high and 46 m (150 ft) wide, set upon the summit of a small mountain. On weekends and holidays a funicular takes visitors to the base of the cross where you may investigate the plinth adorned by four enormous figures.

Equally spectacular is the underground **Basilica**. Carved 240 m (786 ft) deep into the granite mountain, it is reached via a tunnel and opens out into a gigantic dome that is almost directly under the cross outside. The tombstones of Franco and José Antonio Primo de Rivera, founder of the Falangist Party, occupy a privileged position. A series of Flemish tapestries dating from 1553 decorates the church, and ossuaries in the crypt (closed to the public) contain the remains of tens of thousands of the dead, of both sides, from the Civil War.

Segovia

Segovia, 88 km (55 miles) northwest of Madrid, is an unspoiled medieval town that, strategically, sits on a high promontory between two rivers. High on the rocks overlooking the confluence of the rivers is the **Alcázar**, Segovia's fairytale royal castle. Although originally constructed in the 12th and 13th centuries, much of it dates from the next

Segovia's 1st-century Roman aqueduct was built without using a drop of cement.

two centuries. It became a royal favorite — Isabella left from here to be proclaimed queen — but was converted to a Royal Artillery School in the late 18th century and was largely rebuilt after a fire in 1862. Today, it is home to an interesting museum, and you can climb the 152 steps to the top of the tower for spectacular views.

The towering **cathedral** was begun in 1525, after the original one — on a different site — was destroyed during the Communidades War. As a consequence it is the last of the great Spanish cathedrals to be built in the Gothic style. Fine stained-glass windows illuminate the interior.

Segovia is most famous, though, for the **Roman aqueduct**, both a work of art and a triumph of engineering. Dating from the first or second century A.D., it has 165 arches covering a length of 728 m (2,392 ft) and it reaches 28 m (92 ft) in height. Amazingly, the granite stones are held together by nothing but their own weight.

Segovia has an array of other interesting churches, monasteries and museums, the most interesting of which is a small church just outside the town, almost within the shadow of the **Alcázar**. The **Vera Cruz** church dates from the 13th century and was probably founded by the Knights Templar. Having 12 sides, it is unique in Spain but similar to many other churches the knights founded in Portugal. Among museums, the new **Esteban Vicente Contemporary Art Museum** contains some 142 works by the Spanish-born, New York artist.

☞ BARCELONA AND ENVIRONS

Of Phoenician origins, Barcelona flourished under the Romans, and remains of the walls constructed during that era are still visible in the city's so-called Gothic Quarter; finds from the Roman town are on display in the City History Museum. The period of Visigothic rule saw a decline in importance and although the Moors swept across the Iberian peninsula in the early 8th century they were unable to control this area for long. In 801, following its recapture by the Franks, the city was incorporated into Charlemagne's empire as the capital of the Earldom of Barcelona, the most dominant of the Catalan earldoms. For nearly five centuries, unlike in other parts of the country, Barcelona and Catalunya remained Christian, giving this region an entirely different character from the rest of Spain. Subsequently, it was united

Barcelona Highlights

Monastir de Pedralbes: *Baixada del Monestir 9; Tel. (93) 203 92 82; website <museuhistoria.bcn.es>. Bus 22.* The Thyssen-Bornemisza art collection housed in one of Europe's best Gothic cloisters houses. Tuesday–Sunday 10am–2pm. €2.40. (See page 50)

Museu d'Història de la Ciutat: *Plaça del Rei s/n; Tel. (93) 315 11 11; web site <www.museuhistoria.bcn.es>.* Barcelona's history from the 1st century B.C., with a model of the city in the 15th century. Summer Tuesday–Saturday 10am–8pm; Sunday 10am–2pm. €4.80. (See page 48)

Museu Marítimo: *Av. Drassanes s/n; Tel (93) 342 99 20; web site <www.diba.es/mmaritim>.* Full-size vessels and numerous models in the 14th-century royal dockyards. Monday–Sunday 10am–7pm. €5.40. (See page 47)

Museu Nacional d'Art de Catalunya: *Palau Nacional, Montjuïc; Tel. (93) 622 03 60; web site <www.mnac.es>.* Catalonia's impressive national art collection features entire Catalan church interiors and notable Spanish art from the 16th to 18th centuries. Tuesday–Saturday 10am–7pm, Sunday 10am– 2:30pm. €4.80. (See page 49)

Museu Picasso: *Carrer de Montcada 15-23; Tel. (93) 319 63 10; web site <www.museupicasso.bcn.es>.* The most important collection in the world of his early works, major pieces from his Blue and Pink Periods as well as ceramics and engraved works. Tuesday–Saturday 10am–8pm, Sunday 10am–3pm. €3.00. (See page 48)

Poble Espanyol: *Montjuïc; Tel. (93) 322 0326.* Spain in miniature with traditional houses and entertainment. Monday 9am–8pm, Tuesday–Thursday 9am–2am, Friday–Saturday 9am–4am, Sunday 9am–midnight. €6.00. (See page 49)

Sagrada Família: *Plaça Sagrada Família; Tel. (93) 455 02 47. Metro: Sagrada Familia.* Gaudí's mind-boggling unfinished cathedral; for more in the same vein, pick up a free copy of the Gaudí brochure at the tourist office. Open daily 9am–8pm. €4.80. (See page 49)

Aquàrium de Barcelona: *Port Vell; Tel. (93) 221 7474.* Europe's largest aquarium, unveiled in 1998. Weekdays 10am–9pm, holidays and summer until 10pm. (See page 48).

with the kingdom of Aragón in the 12th century, thus ensuing a period of flourishing maritime trade.

Ferdinand and Isabella's wedding, in 1474, united the kingdoms of Castile and Aragón to form the country of Spain as it exists today. However, in the process of centralization the new government attempted to suppress the well-established institutions of this dynamic and strongly independent region. For the next few centuries, Barcelona repeatedly struggled to maintain its unique identity. During the Spanish Civil War it served as the capital of the Republican forces and was one of the last cities to fall to Franco — as a result of which Barcelona was later singled out for harsh reprisals, and even the Catalan language was suppressed. Now, with a well-earned reputation for its architecture and style, Barcelona is the thriving capital of a largely autonomous region where the people openly display a passion for all things Catalan, including their language. The net effect is an ambiance quite different to that in the rest of Spain.

Barcelona is a large city (the second largest in Spain) and its many attractions are widely separated from each other. It helps that there is an excellent public transport system, and the buses and *metro* (subway) will take you most everywhere you need to go. A neat option is the Bus Turistic, which has two routes — the red northern route and blue southern route (with connections at three stops). Each route provides a handy hop-on, hop-off service around all the main sights. Tickets can be purchased on board or at tourist offices. They include discounted admission to many museums and attractions, including the cable car, funicular, and tram rides for Montjuïc and Tibidabo. Also worth considering is the **Barcelona Card**, which can be purchased for periods of 1, 2 or 3 days and offers free public transport as well as over 100 discounts at museums, places of entertainment, shops, restaurants and even the Aerobus (airport bus).

Without doubt **La Rambla**, linking the popular Plaça de Catalunya with the harbor, is Barcelona's most popular street, and a cocktail of attractions unique not only in Spain but also Europe. Everyone comes to walk along its wide tree-lined promenade, with its living statues posing for photographs, its street artists performing impromptu shows, its market stalls and brightly colored flower kiosks, its open-air restaurants and bars. Along its route are numerous places of interest, including the ever-popular **La Boqueria** — the 19th-century covered market that is a city highlight — and the famous **Liceu** opera house (recently rebuilt once again after another disastrous fire). A little farther on, Gaudí's fortress-like **Palau Güell,** on Nou de la Rambla, was built for his major sponsor in 1885. And across La Rambla a passage leads into the café-filled arcades of the fine **Plaça Reial**, adorned by a central fountain and iron lanterns, both designed by Gaudí, and no less than 35 palm trees. Further down, the **Mirador de Colón** — honoring Christopher Columbus — towers over the harbor area and is close to the **Museu Marítimo**, which traces 700 years of Barcelona's maritime history (and is well worth a visit just for the architecture).

Columbus landed at Barcelona in 1493 at the end of his voyage of discovery to the New World.

The harbor area, at the southern end of **La Rambla**, has been completely transformed in recent years. Traditional **golondrinas** boats offer a fun way of seeing the harbor or you can cross the water to the **Port Vell** by way of a wooden promenade to find a modern complex consisting of shops, restaurants, an IMAX theater and the **Aquàrium de Barcelona** — one of Europe's largest and a favorite for children of all ages.

The narrow alleyways and historic buildings of the **Barri Gòtic** cluster around the imposing **Catedral**. The third on the site, this dates from the 13th century but with a 19th-century façade. In the square outside you will see performances of the Catalan national dance on summer weekends; there is also a graceful garden cloister. Nearby are two fascinating museums: the **Museu d'Història de la Ciutat** (City History Museum) and the **Museu Frederic Marès**, with its eclectic miscellany of religious objects and art from around the world. Among the galleries on Carrer de Montcada, the **Museu Picasso** is the city's most popular museum. Be sure, also, to pop into the **El Xampanyet** bar at No. 22 where, besides delicious *tapas*, a refreshingly light, sparkling champagne-like *cava* is served.

The pure, Gothic beauty of the 14th-century **Santa María del Mar** church can be seen at the bottom of Montcada. To the east, the spacious, green expanse of the **Parc Ciutadella**, its name derived from an 18th-century prison torn down with much glee in 1869, encompasses paths, gardens, and ponds, and an elaborate Gaudí fountain. It also has the **Museum of Modern Art**, and one of Europe's better zoos where the star resident is **Copito de Nieve** (Snowflake), the world's only albino gorilla in captivity.

Barcelona's historic Jewish community once lived on the slopes of **Montjuïc** (Hill of the Jews), which looms up behind the harbor, crowned by the 17th-century **Castillo de Montjuïc** and reached by cable-car, funicular or bus. The castle offers spectacular views of the city and also houses a military museum. Other attractions clinging to the city's steep hillsides include the **Parc Atraccions Montjuïc** fun fair; witty abstract art in the form of the **Fundació Joan Miró**; facilities left from the 1992 Olympic Games including the main stadium, swimming pools and the **Torre de Calatrava** that became one of the symbols of those games; and the **Poble Espanyol** (Spanish Village), which showcases Spanish architecture and traditions with miniature replicas of palaces,

Gaudí's eccentric spires crown Barcelona's unique but unfinished Sagrada Familia cathedral.

castles, and churches, plus artisans' workshops, concerts, and evening flamenco performances. Art lovers should not miss the world-class collections of Romanesque and Gothic art displayed in the **Museu Nacional d'Art de Catalunya** (Catalan Art Museum).

Of course, Barcelona is also famous for Gaudí's unique and eccentric architectural designs. The largest of these is the surrealistic **Sagrada Família** (Holy Family) church. An unfinished masterpiece started in 1882 (and still in progress), its 100-m (330-ft) towers are local landmarks. Other Gaudían highlights include tours of the **Casa Milà** rooftops at Passeig de Gràcia 92; the façade of **Casa Battló** down the street at No. 43; and the fascinating **Parc Güell**, with its colorful tile mosaics.

On the western edge of the city, the beautiful **Monastir de Pedralbes** deserves a special mention. Founded by Queen Elisenda in 1326, it has a charming cloister and an exceptional selection of paintings on loan from the Thyssen-Bornemisza art collection. Last, but by no means least, the popular amusement park at **Tibidabo** combines the best in old- and new-technology rides, offering spectacular views from its perfect perch on a 542-m (1,778-ft) high peak in the western hills overlooking Barcelona.

AROUND BARCELONA

☛ **Montserrat**

Just 40 km (25 miles) northwest of Barcelona, and easily reached by train and cable car, the monastery of Montserrat sits on the ridge of a highly unusual rock formation 1,135 m (3,725 ft) above the Llobregat river valley. This is the spiritual home of Catalonia and one of Spain's most important pilgrimage sites thanks to the monastery's Black Madonna — *La Moreneta* — a statue said to have been made by St Luke and brought to Barcelona by St Peter. In 1808, Napoleon's troops destroyed the original 12th-century monastery and the present building dates from 1874. Montserrat is still an active monastery; visitors may only enter the beautiful Gothic cloister, the basilica, and the museum. A highlight of any visit is a recital by the famous Escalonia Boys' Choir (daily at 12:45pm), while the **museum** features art by El Greco, Picasso, and modern

Catalan artists, as well as inter-esting archaeological treasures. Sadly, rampant commercialism has invaded Montserrat's hal-lowed grounds, though it is easy to escape the crowds by following one of the four well-signposted hermitage walks through Montserrat's magnifi-cent protected mountain park-land. One of these goes to the **Santa Cova** (the Holy Cave) where La Moreneta was allegedly discovered).

Poblet

Travel 133 km (83 miles) west of Barcelona to find the largest and best-preserved Cistercian monastery in Europe. The

Catalonia's medieval monarchs lie buried in Poblet's Gothic chapel.

medieval monastery and fortress of Poblet was founded in 1151 by the Count of Barcelona, Ramon Berenguer, as a gesture of thanksgiving for the reconquest of Catalonia. Poblet's façade is a majestic sight, and once inside a guided tour leads past the wine cellars, library, chapter house, and refectory into the Romanesque and Gothic-style church and its spacious rose-garden cloister.

Tarragona

This site, 95 km (60 miles) south of Barcelona, was home to ancient Iberian tribes, but it was the Romans, in the third cen-tury B.C., who established it as an important military and political headquarters. Tarraco, as it was then known, quickly grew to a population of 30,000 and minted its own currency. By 27 B.C., it was the capital of Tarraconensis, the largest Roman province on the Iberian peninsula. The town now has some of the finest Roman remains to have survived in Spain, including the city walls, the amphitheater, and an aqueduct.

The Rambla Vella (Old Rambla) neatly divides Tarragona in half. To the north is the old walled city, while to the south is the Rambla Nova (New Rambla) and the newer part of town. At the end of the Rambla Vella the **Balco del Mediterrani** looks down onto Tarragona's commercial port, one of the busiest in the Mediterranean. The adjacent port is worthy of a visit for its fish restaurants.

To get a glimpse of the old city, you can take a walk along the **Passeig Arqueològic**. This follows the top of the old city walls, which enclose a maze of charming medieval streets. The upper levels of the ramparts were originally built by the Romans above huge cyclopean boulders, supposedly placed

Gladiators and Christian martyrs once fought to the death in Tarragona's ancient Roman amphitheater.

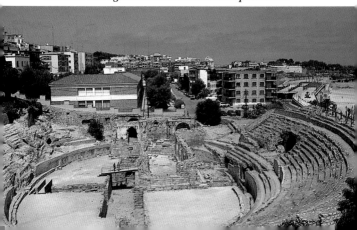

there by Iberian tribes in the sixth century B.C. In this part of town, the **Museu Arqueològic**, Plaça del Rei, hosts a modern, well-designed exhibition of delicate mosaics and other ancient artifacts. Next door, the **Pretori Romà** (Roman Praetorium), is thought to have been part of the original complex belonging to the provincial administration. It was restored in the Middle Ages and today houses the atmospheric **Museu d'Història** (History Museum). Walking from here towards the sea brings you to the ruins of both the Roman **amphitheater**, built into the hillside and the 12th-century **Santa María del Miracle** church. Gladiators fought here and Spain's first Christian martyr died here in A.D. 259.

Medieval Tarragona's pride and joy is its **cathedral**, the largest in Catalonia, founded in 1171 but not consecrated until 1333. The 12th- to 13th-century cloister is an attraction in its own right, while the **Museu Diocesà** has a fine collection of art treasures and Flemish tapestries.

Tarragona's most important ancient site beyond the old city walls, the **Necròpoli i Museu Paleocristià** (Necropolis and Paleo-Christian Museum), stands at the site of the city's early Christian burial ground. Excavations have uncovered over 2,000 graves; you will find the best archaeological discoveries displayed in the museum.

Tarragona's most impressive Roman monument, the first-century **Pont del Diable**, is some 4 km (2½ miles) north of the town center, off the N240 towards Lleida (Lérida). The "Devil's Bridge" is actually a perfectly preserved two-story aqueduct, which spans 217 m (712 ft) and rises to a height of 27 m (88 ft) above the ground.

ANDALUCÍA

Andalucía is the southernmost autonomous region of Spain, stretching from the Atlantic and Portuguese border in the west to the Mediterranean south of Murcia in the east. It consists of eight provinces: Huelva, Cádiz, Málaga, Granada and Almería west to east along the coastline, and Sevilla, Córdoba and Jaén landlocked to the north. It has a magnificent array of scenery, including the Sierra Nevada — the highest peaks in Spain — the alluvial plains of the Guadalquivir river, the deserts of Almería and the *pueblos blancos* (white villages) of the interior. Epitomized by its bullfighting and flamenco dancing, Andalucía is considered by many to be the soul of Spain, and it is home to historic cities whose names — Sevilla, Córdoba and Granada — and histories resonate around the world.

☞ Sevilla

Sevilla was already a thriving riverside settlement when Julius Caesar arrived in Spain in 45 B.C. but under the Romans it developed into a major town. Two Roman emperors — Hadrian and Trajan — were born in nearby Itálica. Subsequently capital of the Visigoths and then of a Moorish *taifa*, Sevilla finally fell to King Ferdinand III in

1248. A monopoly of trade with the New World brought the city to its peak during the Golden Age. "Madrid is the capital of Spain," the saying went, "but Sevilla is the capital of the world." Without doubt Sevilla, the capital of Andalucía and Spain's fourth largest city, is the most important

Sevilla's tranquil Alcázar gardens are a masterpiece of Moorish garden design.

city in the region. And its name alone is evocative of bullfighting, flamenco, the operatic temptress Carmen and many icons that represent Spain in visitors' minds. It is also one of the most beautiful cities in the world.

The city's two most prominent monuments are located around the Plaza del Triunfo. The **cathedral**, the largest Gothic church in the world and third largest of its kind — only St Peter's in Rome and St Paul's in London are bigger — was begun in 1401 after the great mosque was razed. The new building followed the

Once a minaret, Sevilla's Giralda tower now graces the city's huge cathedral.

ground plan of the old mosque, accounting for its unusual broad, rectangular form. Massive without, and richly decorated within, the cathedral contains over 30 chapels, including the central **Capilla Mayor** with its Flemish Plateresque altarpiece, and the **Capilla Real** (Royal Chapel), last resting place of Ferdinand III, the "King-Saint" who delivered Sevilla from the hands of the infidel. The stunning altar screen is overlaid with 3,500 kilos (7,716 pounds) of gold. Cristobal Colón (Christopher Columbus) is interred in the ornate 19th-century sarcophagus by the south entrance. His remains were transferred to Sevilla from Havana in 1898, when Cuba won its independence from Spain. On the north side of the cathedral is the **Patio de los Naranjos** (Court of the Orange Trees), the ceremonial courtyard of the

Sevilla Highlights

Cathedral and Giralda Tower: *Calle Alemanes; Tel. (95) 421 49 71.* The world's largest Gothic church is partnered by the landmark Giralda Tower, a former minaret turned lofty city symbol. Open Monday to Saturday 10am–5pm, Sunday cathedral 2pm–6pm, Giralda 10am–4pm. €4.20, free on Sunday. (See page 55).

Alcázar: *Plaza del Triunfo; Tel. (95) 422 71 63 or web site <www.patronato-alcazarsevilla.es>.* Mudéjar palace with beautiful gardens. Open Tuesday to Saturday 9:30am–7pm, Sunday and holidays 9:30am–5pm. €4.20. (See page 56).

Casa de Pilatos: *Calle Aguilas; Tel. (95) 422 52 98.* Elegant Renaissance palace townhouse supposedly modeled on Pontius Pilate's house in the Holy Land. Open daily 9am–7:30pm. €6.00. (See page 57).

Museo de Bellas Artes: *Plaza del Museo; Tel. (95)422 07 90.* A fine collection of Spanish and foreign paintings. Open Wednesday to Saturday 9am–8pm, Tuesday 3–8pm, Sunday 9am–2pm. €1.50. (See page 57).

old mosque with its original ablutions fountains. The bell tower of the cathedral, the celebrated **Giralda** tower — Sevilla's most famous landmark — dates from 1184, and was the original mosque's minaret. The exterior is beautifully decorated with typical *sebka* design work while the interior has a series of 35 gently rising ramps (designed for horses to climb — Ferdinand III rode his horse to the top following the Reconquest in 1248) leading to an observation platform 70 m (230 ft) in the air and offering a tremendous panorama across the city.

The **Alcázar** is a major monument of mid-14th century Mudéjar architecture, combining Moorish, Gothic, and

Renaissance elements. Built by Moorish craftsmen under Christian rule, during the reign of Pedro the Cruel, the rambling palace and its several courtyards incorporate fragments of an earlier Moorish fortress, and blend Christian motifs with Moorish designs. Not to be missed are the extensive and beautiful gardens, an oasis of tranquility in this perpetually busy city.

Nearby, on the banks of the river, is another of Sevilla's icons. The Moorish **Torre del Oro** (Tower of Gold) is named after the gold-colored tiles that once covered the walls of this early 13th-century tower — all that remains of Sevilla's medieval fortifications.

Bordering on the Alcázar, the labyrinthine streets of the **Barrio de Santa Cruz** exude history and charm. On the border of this district, more Mudéjar sensations await in the 16th-century **Casa de Pilatos**.

Other places not to miss are the **Hospital de la Caridad** (Charity Hospital), the **Plaza de España**, the **Bullfighting Museum and Plaza de Toros**, the **Museo de Bellas Artes** (Fine Arts Museum) and the site of Roman **Itálica**, 10 km (6 miles) to the northwest.

Córdoba

Córdoba was the largest city in Roman Spain, the capital of the province of Batik, and birthplace of Seneca the Younger, philosopher and tragedian. But its golden era was between the mid-eighth and very early 11th centuries when it was the center of the great medieval Caliphate of Córdoba. As one of the world's largest and most cultured cities, the splendid capital of the western Islamic Empire had the first university and the earliest street lighting in Europe.

The city now is dominated by the greatest surviving monument from that period. The Great Mosque, known as

La Mezquita, was begun in 786 but it was enlarged three times before attaining its present size, covering an area of 2 hectares (5 acres), in 987. Córdoba was reconquered in 1236, and two small Christian chapels were added in 1258 and 1260. In the early 16th century Carlos V constructed a Christian Cathedral in the center of the mosque. With its heavy ornamentation, its blaze of color and its human images in paint, stone and wood, this contrasts greatly with the understated simplicity — and lack of human images — of Islamic design. Set in the southeast wall, is the splendid 10th century **mihrab**, lined with marble and gold mosaics, and the **maksourah**, the enclosure where the caliph attended to his prayers.

A Christian king, Alfonso XI, built Córdoba's Alcázar de los **Reyes Cristianos,** and there are pleasant patios, Roman relics, terraced gardens, and wonderful views from the

ramparts. Ferdinand and Isabella received Columbus and planned the invasion of Granada while they were in residence here.

Also well worth a visit are the 14th-century **syna-gogue** in the **Barrio de la Judería** (Jewish Quarter), the 16th-century **Palacio de los Marquéses de Viana**, with its 13 flower-filled patios that are so

Córdoba's Great Mosque is one of the world's finest Islamic structures.

typical of Córdoba, the **Plaza de la Corredera** dating from the 17th century and the only Castilian style plaza in Andalucía, the **Museo Arqueológico** and the **Museo Taurino**. Look, also, for the unusual **Plaza del Potro**, home to the **Museo de Bellas Artes** (Fine Arts Museum) and the **Julio Romero de Torres Museum.**

Granada

The Nasrid dynasty rose to power in Granada just as the fortunes of the Spanish Moors were beginning to wane, when Mohammed ben Alhamar established his capital here in 1232, after Ferdinand III had forced him from Jaén. Two years later, Moors fleeing from the newly vanquished Sevilla swelled the population, which had already been augmented by refugees from Córdoba. These industrious Moors set about making Granada the grandest city of Andalucía, creating the sumptuous hilltop palace of the Alhambra. Granada was the last of the great Moorish kingdoms of Andalucía to be re-conquered, having survived more than 250 years longer than the others, and King Boabdil's surrender to the Catholic Monarchs in January 1492 marked the end of the Muslim Empire in Spain.

The second most visited monument in Spain, the world-famous **Alhambra** (meaning "The Red") takes its name from the red-brown bricks used in the construction of its outer walls. Rising precipitously above the deep gorge of the Río Darro, these have the towering — and often snow-covered — peaks of the Sierra Nevada as a backdrop.

There are four main areas to explore: the **Alcazaba, Casa Real Vieja**, **Casa Real Nueva** and the **Generalife**. The **Alcazaba** (fortress) is the oldest section with towers dating from as far back as mid-13th century. From the top of the **Torre de la Vela** (Watchtower) there are excellent views over the modern city below. The **Casa Real Vieja** (Old Royal Palace), actually a combination of palaces, is what most people come to see. The intricacy, delicacy and bountiful beauty of the designs here create a visual impression that is beyond mere words. The highlights are the **Salón de Embajadores** (Hall of the Ambassadors), or royal audience chamber, one of the most sumptuously ornamented rooms in the Alhambra; the **Patio de los Leones**, the name of which derives from the splashing fountain in the center upheld by 12 stone lions; the **Torre de las Damas** (Tower of the Ladies); and the old bathing area. The **Casa Real Nueva** (new Royal Palace) was commissioned in 1527 by Carlos V; square on the outside, it has a surprisingly elegant two-story circular patio inside. It houses The **Museo Nacional de Arte Hispano-Musulmán** (Museum of Hispano-Moorish Art) and the **Museo de Bellas Artes** (Fine Arts Museum). The **Generalife** (summer gardens), at the eastern end of the Alhambra fortifications, has a modest summer palace that is surrounded by beautiful terraced gardens, where oleander and roses bloom luxuriantly, and delicate fountains and cascades play among the neatly clipped cypress hedges. Amazingly, this complex was allowed to fall into almost total disrepair over the centuries, and it wasn't until 1870 that it was designated a National Monument.

Facing the Alhambra hill, the **Albaicín**, Granada's oldest and most picturesque quarter, is fun to explore, affording glimpses of the Alhambra between whitewashed houses, outdoor restaurants, and cafés. At the bottom of the hill are some **Arab baths**.

Back down in the city the most prominent monument is the exquisite **Capilla Real** (Royal Chapel), a Renaissance chapel that serves as the mausoleum of the Catholic Monarchs, as well as their daughter, Juana La Loca, and her husband, Felipe El Hermoso. Their mortal remains were interred in the crypt below in 1521, after a ceremonial transfer of their remains from the Alhambra. On show in the **sacristy** are momentos of the Catholic Monarchs, including Ferdinand's sword and Isabella's sceptre and crown, a circle of gold embellished with acanthus scrolls.

Jerez de la Frontera

The largest town in Cádiz, the fame of Jerez is based upon sherry and horses. The English corrupted Jerez to "sherry" and exported the locally produced wine.

Learn about the art of sherry-making and enjoy a glass at a Jerez bodega.

Several of the many **bodegas** (wineries) in Jerez welcome tourists to their dark, aromatic halls, and offer free tastings. As for the horses, the **Real Escuela Andaluza de Arte Ecuestre** (Royal Andalucían School of Equestrian Art) puts its star pupils through a beautifully choreographed dressage show at midday every Thursday and on Tuesday between March and October, and there are weekday training sessions. The highlight of the equestrian calendar is the May **Spring Horse Fair**, when the town is full of dandified horses and their even more elaborately dressed riders.

An 11th-century mosque is found inside the **Alcázar** fortress, and the nearby 18th-century **Colegiata** holds a precious image of Christ of the Vineyards. Amongst the

other attractions look especially for the Andalucían Flamenco Center in the distinguished Pemartín Palace and the striking Clock Museum in its own delightful gardens.

Carmona

Carmona has a 5,000-year-old history that dates back to the Neolithic period. It was the Roman era, though, that brought the area prosperity and wealth, and the **Museo y Necropolis** is the largest Roman necropolis outside of Rome itself. Carmona was never under feudal rule, and was protected as a "Crown" city, consequently it has an extraordinary number of palaces, mansions, convents and churches. It also has two formidable gates that linked the old *card maxim* (the Roman road).

Ronda

Dramatically clinging to a cliff-top 150 m (500 ft) above the Tajo gorge, Ronda was both an Iberian and, later, a Roman settlement whilst under the Moors it proved impregnable for seven centuries. The Puente Nuevo spans the gorge, which connects the new center with the old town from where Ronda's Moorish kings and its Christian conquerors ruled at the **Palacio de Mondragón**. Behind a Renaissance portal, the elegant courtyards, horseshoe arches, and Arabic inscriptions reveal the origins of this stately structure. The town's main mosque survives a short walk away as the **Santa María la Mayor** church.

The rules of modern bullfighting were codified at Ronda's late-18th century bullring, one of the oldest in Spain.

Back across the bridge, seek out the neo-classical **Plaza de Toros** (bullring), one of the oldest in Spain and venerated as the cradle of the *corrida* (see page 139). It was a Ronda man, Francisco Romero, who spelled out the rules of bullfighting in the 18th century. There's a small museum here that is of interest to the non-aficionado.

Medina Azahara

Eight km (5 miles) west of Córdoba are the ruins of the intriguing Medina Azahara city/palace, commissioned in 936 by Abdel-Rahman III in honor of his favorite concubine Al Zahra (The Flower). It had a short life because it was razed with the breakup of the Caliphate of Córdoba in the very early 11th century. For nearly 900 years it was left in ruins, and not until 1910 did the slow work of excavation begin. This still continues, but reconstructed royal apartments give some impression of the original magnificence of this sumptuous complex of baths, schools, gardens, and stately apartments built on three terraces.

Alcalá la Real

Known in Roman times, this was a Moorish fortified city from the early eighth century and remained a strategic bastion until the reconquest of Granada in 1492, after which further Christian monuments were added. The **Fortaleza de la Mota**, on the summit at 1,033 m (3,389 ft), is an amazing complex combining Moorish and Christian influences, along with spectacular views. A particular fascination, and one both beautiful and gruesome, is the semi-ruined church whose floor has been partly excavated leaving tombs with bones and skulls exposed.

Baeza and Úbeda

These beautifully preserved twin towns, separated by a small valley, flourished as Christian strongholds during the Reconquest. **Baeza**, with more than 50 listed historical buildings, is the smaller of the two. **Úbeda** is just as engaging, and its showcase square, the **Plaza Vázquez de Molina**, is surrounded by a host of magnificent Renaissance palaces and churches. The town hall is housed in the **Palacio de las Cadenas** (Palace of Chains), so called for the chains round its forecourt, and the **Sacra Capilla del Salvador** (Chapel of the Holy Saviour) is the town's finest church.

THE COSTAS

From the Costa Brava at the eastern end of the Pyrenees all the way round to the Costa de la Luz and the border with Portugal, the famous Spanish *costas* attract millions of vacationers every year. The coastline stretches for some 2,500 km (1,562 miles) from the sheltered Mediterranean to the blustery Atlantic. There are rocky coves and glorious stretches of golden sand, family resorts, and jet-set ports. In spite of the much-reported ravages of extensive development and building, you can still find many charming spots along the coast. The *costas* — not now always as cheap and cheerful as they once were — offer a sun-and-fun atmosphere that will always be a major attraction.

The Costa Brava was the birthplace of surrealist artist, Salvador Dalí.

The Costa Brava

Stretching from the French border to just north of Barcelona, this is perhaps the prettiest coastline in Spain. Package tourism arrived here in the early 1960s, but the cliffs and coves of the "Wild Coast" still conceal a handful of traditional fishing villages and secluded beaches in the north of the region. You will find the major tourism development concentrated in the south (at the Lloret de Mar resort, for instance).

Cadaqués may look like a typical whitewashed fishermen's village, but it attracts a distinctly atypical crowd of chic, monied vacationers. Although it is still a working port, without a decent beach, the village has developed into something of an artists' haunt. In fact, Salvador Dalí built a modest retreat here on the edge of Cadaqués at Port Lligat in 1929. On top of the old town, the 17th-century **church**, with a rich altarpiece, was built as a replacement for its predecessor, burned down in 1543 by Barbarossa, the infamous Barbary pirate. Art enthusiasts can admire a selection of modern masters in the **Perrot-Moore Museum** (founded by Dalí's ex-secretary). The local Museu d'Art also includes works by household-name artists.

Ampurias was built by the Greeks, improved by the Iberians, and then greatly expanded by the Romans. The site was perpetually occupied for some 1,500 years. An archaeologist's delight, excavations have uncovered the remains of the villas, temples, and marketplaces of these different civilizations. You will also find lovely sea views. The most sensational find was a statue of Asclepius, the Greek god of

---

Dalí in Figueres

Born in Figueres (Figueras) 30 km (19 miles) west of Cadaqués in 1904, the Surrealist artist Salvador Dalí endowed his hometown with the suitably surreal Teatre-Museu Dalí (closed Monday). The second most visited museum in Spain (after the Prado), it is a typically outrageous Daliesque project. A municipal theater was gutted, its stage filled with bizarre sculptures, and an ancient Cadillac supporting a statue of a gilt-breasted Amazon was parked on the patio. There are giant models of hens' eggs on the battlements, a roofline topped by a geodesic dome, and Dalí's version of the Sistine Chapel — a homage to Mae West with her lips replaced by a voluptuous red sofa. Shocks and jokes aside, the museum represents an intriguing cross-section of Dalí's work.

Tossa de Mar's pretty bay and beautifully sited medieval castle proved a magnet to such artists as Mark Chagall.

medicine, which was sculpted in marble from an Athenian quarry. The original has been removed to Barcelona, but a copy stands in the ruined temple. The on-site **museum** displays local finds, from ceramics and jewels to household items and weapons.

Tossa de Mar, in the dramatic cliff country south of Bagur, was an artists' colony before it metamorphosed into a fully developed international resort. The town remains surprisingly attractive, its **Vila Vella** (Old Town) enclosed by brooding 12th-century walls and guarded by three great towers. The **museum** here boasts paintings by Marc Chagall and other artists who visited the town.

Gerona (Girona) is the inland gateway to the Costa Brava, and is a pleasant day-trip destination from the coast 30 km (20 miles) west. The old town is fun to explore, with its typical medieval streets such as **Carrer de la Força,** once the heart of the Jewish quarter. Gerona's Gothic **cathedral** is said to have the widest nave in the world at 22 m (72 ft), and the treasury, the **Museu Capitular,** is crammed with precious gold and silverwork, rare illuminated manuscripts, statuary, and tapestries. Close by, the 12th-century **Banys Arabs** (Arab Baths) are the best preserved in Spain after those in Granada.

The Costa Dorada

Stretching from just north of Barcelona to the Ebro Delta, the Costa Dorada derives its name from the fine golden (*daurada*) sand beaches that stretch almost without a break for 241 km (150 miles) south of Barcelona. (The city of Tarragona, midway down the coast, is covered in **Around Barcelona** – see page 51).

Sitges, a sophisticated and attractive resort, retains much of its old-world charm and the old town is built around a promontory. Surmounting this, the neo-Gothic **Palau Mar i Cel** (Palace of the Sea and Sky) houses a fine collection of paintings and *objets d'art* from around the world, plus romantic sea views through picture windows. Adjacent, **Cau Ferrat** ("Iron Lair") houses one of Spain's most exquisite small museums. Works by El Greco and Picasso, ceramics, crystal, and much more are imaginatively displayed. Another good museum is the **Museu Romàntic**, in an aristocratic mansion lavishly decorated in 19th-century style.

Salou, by far the biggest resort on the Costa Dorada, has few pretensions. It is a well-ordered, no-frills playground for north European package vacationers, offering them huge beaches and a good range of facilities and entertainment. Salou also boasts a huge theme park, **Port Aventura**, which promises a journey of adventure through exotic lands, plus all sorts of rides, restaurants, and live entertainment. During the early evening, crowds assemble to watch the town's **illuminated fountain**, designed by Carlos Buigas, who is also renowned for the famous "dancing fountains" in Barcelona.

Cambrils, Salou's more classy neighbor, is an attractive fishing port turned resort that has a long seafront and a charming oddity in its large fleet of *bous* — small boats that carry outsize lamps when they go out to fish at night. The fish caught by these vessels supply the many good restaurants along the waterfront

The Ebro Delta

The Ebro Delta is the largest of Catalonia's wetlands and, after France's famous Camargue, the most important aquatic environment in the western Mediterranean. It is a major breeding ground for waders, waterfowl, and sea birds. Some 7,700 hectares (19,000 acres) of the delta wetlands have been set aside as a protected National Park, making this a

The lagoons, sandbanks, and marshes of the Ebro Delta are home to thousands of birds and rare aquatic species.

true birdwatcher's paradise. There is a tourist office at **Deltebre** that can supply general information, maps, and details of boat excursions and bird- watching sites. Non-birdwatchers can enjoy the wide-open spaces, the glittering green rice paddies (the basic ingredient for *paella* is grown here), and glimpses of the sleepy rural lifestyle.

Tortosa held a key strategic role for centuries as the last major town before the sea. Guarding the Ebro river, its fortress at the top of the town, **La Zuda**, was built by the Moors. Later it became a royal residence of the Aragónese kings. The **cathedral** in the old town was built between the 14th and 16th centuries, and is a fine example of Catalan Gothic.

The Costa del Azahar

From the Ebro Delta to Denia, the "Orange Blossom Coast" begins south of the Tarragona provincial border and stretches for 112 km (70 miles) down a section of coast well endowed with beaches backed by olive orchards and the citrus groves after which the coast is named.

Peñíscola, picturesque and crowned by a medieval castle, is built on a rocky promontory jutting out into the sea. The **castle**, built by the Knights Templar on the ruins of a Moorish fortress, has two claims to fame: Pope Benedict XIII found asylum here after being dismissed from his position until his death in 1423; and the castle featured in the film *El Cid*, starring Charlton Heston. There's a **museum** and terrific sea views from the restored ramparts.

Sagunto (Roman Saguntum) underwent a nine-month siege by the Carthaginian general Hannibal in 219 B.C. that ignited the Second Punic War. The inhabitants set fire to the city and themselves to avoid capture, but when Saguntum was eventually retaken, the Romans redeveloped it on a grand scale. Today, Sagunto's Roman monuments include the heavily restored Roman theater. Nearby, a modest archaeological museum exhibits Iberian, Roman, and medieval relics. From the hilltop acropolis, known as Castell de Sagunt, there are sweeping views that reach over the citrus orchards to the sea.

Valencia

Founded by the Romans in 138 B.C., Valencia later prospered as the capital of a far-flung Moorish kingdom until El Cid briefly re-captured it at the end of the 11th century. But it wasn't until 1238 that Jaime I, El Conquistador (whose banner and sword can be seen in the **Museo Historico Municipal**) finally reconquered the city and proclaimed the

Kingdom of Valencia. Today, Valencia is Spain's third largest city and most of its monuments are within the area bounded by the Turia Gardens (once a river) and the railway station.

The **cathedral** was started in 1262 but — with most parts dating from the 14th and the 15th centuries — it is a patchwork of various architectural styles. Its

Peñíscola's promenade is the perefct place for a stroll in the sun.

The medieval Serrano Tower forms an impressive gateway to Valencia.

landmark octagonal Gothic tower, known as the Miguelete or Micalet, is a symbol of the city and if you climb the 207 steps the view from the 64-m (210-ft) summit is spectacular.

Valencia is surrounded by over 2,300 acres of irrigated land (*huerta*) and for over 1,000 years disputes have been settled by the **Tribunal de Aguas** (Water Council). This is a group of eight men who meet every Thursday at midday outside the Door of the Apostles of the cathedral; business is conducted verbally in Valenciano (the local language) with all decisions being final.

Valencia's **La Longa** (Silk Exchange) dates from the late 15th century. Besides being one of the finest secular Gothic structures in Europe it is also famous for its Hall of Pillars where finely crafted helicoidal columns curve graciously to the roof. Across the street the Modernist-style **central market**, built between 1910 and 1926, is an irregular eight-sided building where you will find an enticing array of meat, fish, vegetables and fruit. Outside, look for stalls that sell *paella* pans in a huge range of sizes.

Of Valencia's museums, the recently reopened **Museo Nacional de Cerámica**, housed in an astonishing old palace, is a gem and has assembled hundreds of glorious glazed tiles (*azulejos*) among its treasures. The city's major art collection, at the **Museo Provincial de Bellas Artes**, exhibits paintings by Bosch, El Greco, Goya, and Velázquez, and has a definitive collection of 15th-century Valencian art.

The **Serrano** and **Quart** towers are formidable reminders that such defensive fortifications were more than needed in centuries past. Just outside the city center Valencian architecture is entering the modern age via the city's new **Arts and Sciences Park** (*La Ciudad de las artes y las Ciencias*). The sprawling complex of futuristic buildings and parklands on the southern edge of the city is dedicated to fun and learning. **L'Hemistèric**, a planetarium built in the shape of a gigantic open eye, was designed by Valencian architect Santiago Calatrava, and opened in 1998. Other attractions are the **Art Palace and Science Museum**, also designed by Calatrava, and the **Universal Oceanographic Park**.

Gandía

A town in two parts, Gandía has a busy resort on a vast beach down on the coast and a splendid 14th-century palace tucked away in its inland town center. Birthplace of Duke Francisco de Borja, 16th-century noble turned Jesuit priest, the **Palacio de los Duques** is now a showcase for splendid tapestries, paintings, and antiques, many of them amassed by the pious duke.

The Costa Blanca

The Costa Blanca, which stretches from Denia to La Manga, was named Akra Leuka ("White Headland") by ancient Greek tradesmen who founded a colony here 2,500 years ago. The brilliant light, hot, dry climate and miles of fine, sandy beaches and temperate water make the "White Coast" one of Spain's liveliest tourist zones.

The Northern Beaches

The beaches sprawl to the north and south of the town of **Denia**, named after a Roman temple dedicated to the goddess Diana. Farther south, the family resort of **Jávea** has a fine beach and a pleasant old quarter. **Calpe** is a former fishing village with pleasant sandy beaches in the lee of the **Peñón de Ifach**, an imposing volcanic outcrop. **Altea's** old houses climb steeply to a carefully preserved old quarter, virtually unchanged in the face of the tourist tide, and home to a thriving artistic community.

Benidorm has come to symbolize the worst excesses of package tourism. It has an unattractive towering skyline that stretches far back from the 7 km (4 mile) beach, but it does know what the package-tour invaders want — and provides it non-stop around the clock without pretension. Surprisingly, the old fishermen's quarter still exists, a major saving grace. Likewise, there are sweeping views from the attractive **Balcón de Mer** encompassing the town's truly impressive crescent of beaches backed by the wind-sculpted mountains. Just offshore, boats visit the **Isla de Benidorm**, a bird sanctuary. The Moorish eagles' nest village-fortress of **Castell de Guadalest**, which is situated 28 km (17 miles) northwest, is another favorite excursion. Adding to its attractions, the new **Terra Mitica** theme park has opened south of Benidorm. This takes visitors on a journey through the history of the ancient civilizations of the Mediterranean, including Egypt, Greece, Rome and Iberia.

Alicante, with a population of over a quarter of a million, is a typical bustling Mediterranean port with a splendid palm-lined promenade, lots of outdoor cafés, and the

Alicante's long sandy beaches, palm-lined esplanades and seafront cafés make it a popular holiday destination.

spacious beach of Playa Postiguet. Alicante's imposing clifftop **Castillo de Santa Barbara** was built on the site of a Carthaginian fort founded in the third century B.C. Below the castle the old **Barrio de Cruz** is atmospheric and full of character. Here you will find the baroque façade of the 14th-century church of **Santa María** next to the **Museo de Arte de Siglo XX** (Museum of 20th-Century Art), focusing on the Spanish artists Miró, Picasso, and Dalí.

Elche (Elx), just inland, is famous for its **date plantation**, the largest in Europe. The **Palacio de Altamira**, a former royal holiday residence, is now occupied by an archaeological museum that has a replica of the famous *Dama de Elche* sculpture (the original is in Madrid).

Costa Cálida

The most famous stretch of the Costa Cálida (the "Warm Coast"), which forms the southern portion of the Costa

The towering baroque façade of Murcia's elegant cathedral.

Blanca, is the **Mar Menor** (Little Sea), a vast lagoon almost completely sheltered from the Mediterranean by a 22-km (14-mile) spit. High-rise resort facilities have multiplied on the sandy breakwater, including the famous Club La Manga vacation complex.

Cartagena, named after the Carthaginians, is an important port and naval base with a well-protected harbor overlooked by the ruins of the 14th-century **Castillo de la Concepción**. It is worth driving up for the views.

Murcia, the inland capital of the Costa Cálida, is pleasant and prosperous with a pretty old town. The landmark **Catedral de Santa María**, built in the 14th century, is one of Spain's finest, adorned with a fabulous baroque façade. The outstanding **Vélez chapel** is a highlight of the interior, and in the museum there are wood sculptures by Francisco Salzillo (1797–1883), Murcia's greatest artist. There are more of his works in the **Museo Salzillo.** Among Murcia's other museums, the **Museo Provincial de Bellas Artes** (Fine Arts) is the best.

The Costa de Almería

Almería is a modern city that reveals its Moorish origins in the form of the gigantic eighth-century **Alcazaba** fortress, which overhangs the town and port. The city's crenellated outer walls and a section of the turreted ramparts remain

standing among the 35 hectares (87 acres) of ruins. The
waterfront **Paseo de Almería** is ideal for strolling and shopping. Inland from the harbor, the fortified Gothic **cathedral**
was completed in the mid-16th century.

This is Spain's dustbowl. A searing and parched corner of
the Mediterranean coast, development has been kept at bay
until very recently. On the coast are the small, but growing,
resorts of **Mojácar**, **Roquetas da Mar**, and **Garruche**.
Inland, the dramatic, desolate, desert-like landscape is a
favorite with spaghetti-Western film-makers, who have nick-
named it **Mini-Hollywood.**

Costa Tropical

The coastline of the province of Granada is definitely the
most attractive, and the least developed, stretch of Spain's
southern coast, and the stretch between Adra and Motril is a
conservation area. There are no large developments, and few
hotels here; just numerous uncrowded small beaches with
crystal clear water surrounded by the mountains dropping
into the sea. **Motril** sits in the midst of a fertile plain while
the hill of **Salobreña**, just west, is crowned with a magnificent castle. **Almuñécar** is the only other town of any size,
and has an ancient history. A fine **aqueduct** stands as a
monument to the skills of the Roman engineers who
constructed it during the reign of Antoninus Pius in the
second century A.D.

The Costa del Sol

Nerja is the only sizeable resort of note east of Málaga, and
is increasingly popular with vacationers. Its cliff-top **Balcón
de Europa** has an attractive palm-fringed promenade. The
principal attraction is the **Cueva de Nerja**, a truly cavernous
grotto 4 km (2½ miles) east of town. Wall paintings and

Spiritual geometry at Marbella's Mezquita del Rey Abdulaziz mosque.

archaeological finds indicate that the stalactite-encrusted cave — home to the world's longest stalactite at 59 m (195 ft) — has been inhabited since the days of Cro-Magnon man.

Málaga, by far the largest town, is the international gateway to the Costa del Sol with many millions arriving at its airport. It also has a busy harbor overlooked by an **Alcazaba** built by the Moors, now consisting mostly of landscaped ruins and home to a modest archaeological museum. At the top of the hill, the sprawling **Gibralfaro** fort ruins afford spectacular views out to sea and inland to the mountains. Situated a short distance from Málaga's grandiose but rather gloomy cathedral, the former Museo de Bellas Artes in the 16th-century Buenavista Palace has been expanded and converted into a new **Picasso Museum** (opened 2002). Picasso himself was born nearby at Plaza de la Merced 15. The traditional costumes and folk arts displayed in the entertaining **Museo Artes y Costumbres Populares** are well worth a quick detour. They are housed in an inn built in the 17th century near the Guadalmedina river bed.

Torremolinos epitomizes the popular side of the Costa del Sol, with its tower-block hotels stretching well inland away from the famous **La Carihuela** beach, and its *chiringuitos* — small beachside restaurants. So international is the resort that Spanish is almost a second language. The adjacent resort of **Fuengirola** is a similarly popular place, but more family-orientated.

Marbella, though, is the aristocrat of the Costa del Sol resorts, favored by royalty and celebrities for decades. As a result, prices are higher here than anywhere else along the coast, but standards of accommodation, service, and cuisine are superior, too. The 28-km (17-mile) beachfront is built up with expensive hotel complexes, and the spacious **marina** sees more than its fair share of luxury pleasure craft. Across the main road, the **old town** is an attractive warren of twisting streets and alleys full of shops, restaurants, and the odd historic church.

Puerto Banús is Spain's answer to Saint-Tropez. This chic 1970s marina-shopping-entertainment complex is full of tasteful bars, pricey boutiques, classy restaurants, and nightclubs. Its waterfront parade is a catwalk for "beautiful people," many of whom arrive aboard the massive yachts berthed in the harbor.

Estepona, although quite small, is the last of the resorts on the western flank of the coast. It provides all the essentials for a sporty, modern vacation — large luxury hotels, beaches, golf courses and a marina — all in an engaging ambiance. Of Roman origin, Estepona preserves the remains of Moorish fortifications and watchtowers.

The Costa de la Luz

Stretching from the Straits of Gibraltar to the Portuguese border, the Atlantic-facing coast of southern Spain is aptly called the "Coast of Light," because of the crystal clarity of its blue skies. Much loved by artists, it receives a mere

trickle of tourists compared with its neighbour, the bustling Costa del Sol. It is extremely blustery and tourist facilities are limited, but to make up for that, there are long and uncrowded beaches, with easy access to Sevilla and to Spain's best national park (see opposite).

Tarifa, the windsurfing capital of Europe, is just 13 km (8 miles) across the water from North Africa. Morocco's Rif mountains hang on the horizon, and Tangier is often clearly visible. Accomplished windsurfers revel in the strong and consistently windy conditions prevailing at **Tarifa beach**.

Festive lights invite revellers to cast their cares aside and enjoy carnival in Cádiz.

Cádiz

The ancient city of Cádiz, isolated at the end of a very narrow peninsula of land running parallel to the coast, was founded by the Phoenicians in 1100 B.C. and is considered to be Spain's oldest town. In fact, the amazing amalgam of history is not readily apparent, with only the remains of the old Roman Theatre giving much evidence of its age. It was reconquered by Alfonso X in 1262, granted the Monopoly of Trade with Africa by the Catholic Monarchs in 1493 and Columbus departed from here on his second and fourth voyages in 1493 and 1502, respectively. In the latter part of the 16th century it twice came under attack by enemy naval forces, and a period of prosperity ensued when the Casa de Contratación, the monopoly rights for trade with the Americas, was transferred from Sevilla by order of Felipe V in 1717. A century later, on March 19, 1812, and whilst under attack from Napoleon's forces, the national parliament met in the St Felipe Neri church and proclaimed the first Spanish parliament.

The excellent **Museo de Cádiz** exhibits Phoenician and Roman artifacts and paintings by Zurbarán, as well as local crafts. Overlooking the ocean, the baroque and classical **cathedral** gives evidence of an extended construction period between 1772 and 1838, and has a landmark dome that glitters like gold in the sunshine. The curious and unusual **Oratorio de la Santa Cueva** (Church of Santa Cueva) has original underground chapels dating from 1783. However, of more interest is the domed upper chapel added in 1796, whose ceiling is adorned by five spectacular paintings — three of which are fine examples of Goya's work.

Sanlúcar de Barrameda

Situated at the mouth of the Guadalquivir river on the Atlantic coast, Sanlúcar is a popular getaway for families from Sevilla. The town is also famed for vineyards that produce the grapes for Manzanilla, a rich sherry-like fortified wine. The sea breezes are said to supply Manzanilla's distinctive salty tang.

Doñana National Park

The largest and most famous of Spain's national parks, this wild conservation zone is the last great lowland wilderness in southern Europe, and it has three distinct kinds of ecosystem: the **marismas** (salt marshes), the **matorral** (brushwood) and **las dunas** (the sand dunes). Within its boundaries can be found an amazing array of animal, bird and plant life, but what you see is very much dependent upon the time of year you visit. The best way see the park is by bus tour from the visitor center at El Acebuche (Tel. (959) 448711). Be warned, though, that this is a very bumpy and rough ride.

THE COSTA VERDE

Most people have an image of Spain as a land of white sun-baked villages, bullfights and swirling flamenco dancers. However, there is a very different Spain in the north: Cantabria, Asturias and Galicia make up a land of fishermen and farmers, where frequent heavy rain makes for a verdant landscape.

Cantabria

There is plenty of variety in the autonomous region of Cantabria, where the sea and the snow-capped heights of the Picos de Europa can both be covered in a day's excursion. As well as fishing villages, ports, and miles of undeveloped wilderness, the coast of Cantabria also offers several popular summer resorts, such as **Castro Urdiales**, **Laredo**, and **Comillas**.

Santander, the capital of the region, successfully combines the roles of major port and tasteful resort and the beach suburb of **El Sardinero**, with its flower gardens and numerous seafood bars, contributes to the city's holiday atmosphere. Overlooking the sea from the rugged peninsula is the Victorian-style **Magdalena Palace** built for Alfonso XIII as a summer escape, a building of many architectural eccentricities.

Santillana del Mar, just west of Santander, is a perfectly preserved medieval village of gold-colored stone houses, cobbled streets, farmyards, and patrician mansions. None other than Jean-Paul Sartre described it as "the prettiest village in Spain". At the north end of the village is the **Colegiata** (Collegiate Church), dedicated to St Juliana (Santillana is a contraction of her name) whose tomb is inside. Its 12th-century Romanesque **cloister** is a real beauty. In the **convent** at the other end of the village, the **Museo Diocesano** specializes in carvings of saints and angels gathered together from outlying churches.

Santander's links with the sea are remembered at the city's Maritime Museum.

Altamira, 2 km (1½ miles) inland from Santillana, is a cave complex that contains some of the finest and most inspiring prehistoric works of art in Europe. The caves themselves are closed to the public, but there is a museum containing the 30,000-year-old remains of a caveman.

The **Picos de Europa**, just 25 km (16 miles) from the coast, forms part of the wall of the Cantabrian Mountains (Cordillera Cantábrica) that rise to a height of 2,600 m (8,530 ft). The N621 cuts through the dramatic **Desfiladero de la Hermida** gorge along the River Deva

to **Potes**, the main gateway to the eastern Picos. Here you will find fine hiking country, fantastic scenery and good bird-watching. Don't forget to taste some Cabrales — the very pungent local blue cheese.

Asturias

The principality of Asturias is a wild, rugged province known for its fiercely independent people and potent cider. They say that this is the true Spain, because it was the only corner of the country that did not succumb to the Moors when they overran the rest of Spain in the eighth

The verdant foothills and snowy peaks of the Picos de Europa.

century. A band of Christian soldiers, led by local hero Pelayo, descended from the mountains and initiated the Reconquest with a small but significant victory over the Moors at the Battle of Covadonga in A.D. 722. A modern statue of Pelayo stands in the main square of **Covadonga**, and his remains are interred in the **Santa Cueva** (Holy Cave), where he saw a vision of the Virgin Mary that inspired his victory — now a place of pilgrimage.

Oviedo

The Asturian capital is outwardly nondescript, but Oviedo's compact historic center has some fine monuments, plus a host of friendly *sidrarías*, bars serving the potent local cider (*sidra*). The **cathedral** culminates in a flourish with a tall and elaborate Gothic tower, and its **Cámara Santa** (Holy

Chamber), a shrine built by Alfonso II to house holy relics brought from Toledo after it fell to the Moors. Behind the cathedral, the **Museo Arqueológico** is housed in a splendid old palace-convent with a gorgeous plateresque cloister. Beyond the city center, you will find two remarkable examples of Visigothic architecture. A short walk to the northeast, the church of **Santullano**, built in the ninth century, is claimed to be the oldest pre-Romanesque church in Spain. On the wooded slopes 3 km (2 miles) northwest of Oviedo, **Santa María del Naranco** is said to be the reception hall of a palace built for Ramiro I in 842. Just up the hill, part of the former palace chapel, **San Miguel de Lillo**, has beautiful Byzantine-style carvings.

Galicia

Galicia is an autonomous region in the northwestern corner of the Iberian Peninsula, made up of the four provinces of La Coruña, Lugo, Orense and Pontevedra. Rugged and isolated, its coastline is characterized by narrow, rocky *rías* (sea inlets) battered by the Atlantic. Galicia's scalloped coastline is perfect for boating, fishing and, when the sun does shine, swimming. Although the Atlantic coast south from La Coruña has the more spectacular *rías*, the northern

Fishing boats moored in the harbour at Luarca, in the province of Asturias.

indentations, the **Rías Altas**, are home to several unspoiled resort towns and quiet beaches. The medieval village of **Pontedeume** is an old-fashioned resort with a long sandy beach. **Ortigueira** is noted for its fine beach and lush hills. **El Barqueiro**, a picture-postcard fishing village, has a white sand beach and **Viveiro's** monuments offer a contrast to the fishing port and resort ambience. Popular with bathers and fishermen, **Foz** has a particularly mild micro-climate.

La Coruña

The capital of the region and Spain's second largest port is worth a visit for its historic old town and unusual beach, It possesses Spain's oldest lighthouse, the **Torre de Hércules**, said to be the only Roman lighthouse still in operation. Now clad in an 18th-century shell, it affords splendid Atlantic vistas from the lookout 242 steps above-ground. The Spanish Armada sailed for England, and to defeat, from La Coruña's busy **port** in 1588. Behind the port, Avenida de la Marina curves east to the **old town** and its famous **galerias**

(glassed-in terraces) and historic churches and monasteries. The 16th-century **Castillo de San Antón**, guarding the harbor approaches, serves as an archaeological museum.

Santiago de Compostela

The one major town of the region, Santiago is the third holiest shrine

Pilgrims and bishops come to worship at the shrine of the Apostle James in Compostela.

The Legend of St James

Unsubstantiated by the Bible, the legend of St James sprang up in the ninth century when a star is supposed to have directed some Galician shepherds to the Apostle's grave. The story goes that St James brought Christianity to Spain after the death of Christ. When he returned to Judaea, he was martyred by Herod, and his disciples fled with the body in a magical vessel with no sails or crew. It ferried them to the village of Padrón, and the body was buried nearby.

Its "discovery" in the ninth century was hailed as a miracle, and there were several more to follow, including a ghostly sighting of St James on horseback slaying Moors by the thousand at the Battle of Clavijo in 844. These exploits earned him the title "Matamoros" or Moor Slayer. It also elevated him to the position of patron saint of the Reconquest, and of Spain.

The cult of St James spread far and wide, and by the end of the 11th century, the Pilgrim Way (Camino de Santiago) was attracting pilgrims from all over Europe.

in Christendom (after Jerusalem and Rome). Its claim to fame originates from 813, when brilliant stars attracted a peasant called Pelayo to a field where the tomb of the Apostle Saint James (Santiago in Spanish) was revealed to him. Since then pilgrims from all over Europe have traveled the **Camino de Santiago** (Road to Santiago) across northern Spain to this remote corner of the country, at one time the western boundary of the known world. In 1189 Alexander III decreed it a Holy City — a status shared only by Rome and Jerusalem. It is also a lively and attractive place with beautiful buildings, colorful plazas, and a largely pedestrian heart, ideal for sightseeing and relaxing. Wherever you wander in Santiago de Compostela, you will be within sight of a historic church or monastery. There are also plenty of bars and restaurants serving seafood, especially *pulpo* (octopus) fresh from the *rías*.

Construction of the huge and magnificent **cathedral**, replacing an earlier one built on the site where James's remains were found, began in 1075 but was not completed until 1128. Numerous additions and changes have taken place over the centuries, and it was as recently as the 18th century that the beautifully symmetrical double staircase and towers of the Obradoiro façade were completed.

Just inside the main entrance, the 800-year-old **Pórtico de la Gloria** (Door of Glory) is a marvel of Romanesque sculpture by the artist known as Master Mateo. A 13th-century polychrome statue of St James takes the spotlight on the main altar, standing above the crypt where the Saint's remains lie at rest. One thing that should not be missed is the incense burner, the **botafumeiro**, so large that it takes several men to swing it, pendulum fashion, during ceremonial occasions.

Compostela's cathedral still attracts pilgrims from all over the world.

At a right angle to the cathedral's entrance, on Plaza del Obradoiro, the **Hostal de los Reyes Católicos** has a stupendous façade. Founded by Ferdinand and Isabella in 1499, as a pilgrim hostel, this is now a luxurious *parador* (see page 177). For an added insight into local customs, crafts, and folklore, visit the **Museo do Pobo Gallego** housed in the old convent of Santo Domingo, which has very rare triple helicoidal (spiral) staircases, designed to connect all levels of the convent without any supports.

Pontevedra

A strategic port since the Middle Ages, this is one of Galicia's most charming towns with many fine old buildings, gardens, and spacious squares. The city's pride and joy is the plateresque **Iglesia de Santa María la Mayor** in the old fishermen's quarter, whose sculpted **façade** is divided into compartments, each telling a New Testament story.

The patron saint of Pontevedra, the Pilgrim Virgin, is commemorated in the curvaceous 18th-century **Iglesia de la Virgen de la Peregrina**. Nearby, the **Iglesia de San Francisco** was founded in the 14th century and the **provincial museum**, housed in interconnecting historic mansions, offers departments of archaeology and art, and some enlightening exhibits on the Galician seafaring way of life.

Bayona (Baiona)

Bayona has the distinction of being the first town in Spain to learn of Columbus's landing in the New World on 1 March 1493. Today the town is an attractive resort, largely undiscovered by the masses, although Bayona's beaches are small and get crowded in season. A few miles out of the village lies the better and wider beach of **Playa de América**. Bayona's delightful fishing port is full of traditional houses

and tapas bars. Set on a *ría,* the town overlooks a wooded promontory where an ancient castle has been transformed into a *parador* with wonderful views.

Vigo

The last town before Portugal, Vigo is an undistinguished town whose natural harbor has made it the largest port in Spain.

THE BASQUE COUNTRY

The Spanish Basque Country, or País Vasco, is an autonomous region consisting of the three provinces of Alava, Guipúzoca and Vizcaya. Along with their cousins north of the border in France, the Basque people share a near-unpronounceable language, **Euskara**, whose origins cannot be traced. They are fiercely independent of spirit and mind — so

This Crucifix adorns Bayona's castle, now run as a parador hotel.

much so that the ongoing campaign for independence by the terrorist organization ETA has cost many lives over the years. Riots and protests, with varying degrees of violence, can erupt very suddenly. On the other hand, this pretty and normally peaceful region, with many attractive towns, is considered to have the finest cuisine in Spain.

Alava

Vitoria (Gasteiz), the capital of the province and region, was founded by Sancho the Wise, the Navarrese king, in 1181 In

1200 the town passed into the hands of Castile, later growing rich on the wool trade. The medieval town center, laid out in a concentric pattern on the fortified hilltop, is home to the 14th-century **Catedral de Santa María**. Nearby, the **Museo Provincial de Arqueología** features Iron-Age and Roman relics. The prosperous merchants built gracious Renaissance mansions and fine churches such as **San Miguel** on **Plaza de la Virgen Blanco** (White Virgin Square) to the south. A monument here commemorates the Duke of Wellington's 1813 victory in the Wars of Independence. The city's spacious main square, **Plaza de España**, is a classic 18th-century Spanish ensemble, with the town hall on the north side.

Guipúzoca

San Sebastián (Donostia), the capital, is a beautiful city situated around the **Bahía de la Concha** (Shell Bay) — a semi-circle of sandy beaches flanked by two peninsulas. Formerly a fishing and trading port, San Sebastián was elevated to the heights of favored royal seaside resort in the mid-19th century. Having been mostly burnt to the ground on August 13, 1813, during the Wars of Independence, it has little by way of historical monuments, but it does have numerous *belle-époque* villas and buildings. A century later another conflict, the First World War, brought substantial changes to the city as Spain's position of neutrality and San Sebastián's proximity to France (the border is less than 15 miles away) made it a convenient haven for many wealthy people endeavoring to avoid the war. The gracious social life and upmarket style that developed during that period transformed San Sebastián and even now it has a wealthier ambiance than many Spanish towns.

The **Playa de la Concha** dominates the city and makes it a popular family resort, even though little of the golden sands are left exposed at high tide. At one end, directly under Monte Urgull, are the colorful streets of the **Parte Vieja** (Old Quarter), radiating from the arcaded **Plaza de la Constitución**. The atmosphere still recalls something of an old-time fishing village, and the narrow streets are the focus for the early evening walkabout, when locals and visitors cram the multitude of bars and restaurants. The city's oldest church, **San Vicente**, is also to be found in this area, as is the **Museo San Telmo**, which displays the municipal art collections and has sections on local history and crafts. Not far from the fishing port, from where there are summer-season boat trips to the **Isla de Santa Clara** in the bay, the church of **Santa María** has an ornate baroque façade. If you want to learn more about Basque seafaring traditions, including whaling, take a look around the aquarium at the end of the harbor.

Vizcaya

Bilbao is the capital of the province and the industrial heartland of the Basque Country. For the most part, it is just a busy industrial city, but the thriving central district with broad boulevards and leafy parks and the **Casco Viejo** (Old Quarter) are pleasant exceptions.

Until very recently the city had no real attractions to offer, but that changed in October 1997 when the **Museo Guggenheim**, designed by California-based architect Frank Gehry, was inaugurated. This massive and decidedly futuristic structure, funded primarily by the Basque government, is now one of Bilbao's foremost landmarks, rising dramatically beside the banks of the Nervión. Inside, spacious galleries accommodate works predominantly from the 1950s to the present day, including works from the renowned Guggenheim collections of New York and Venice. In addi-

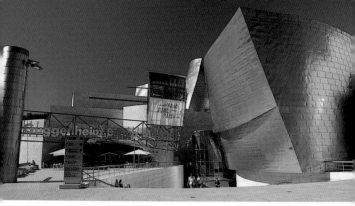

A work of art in itself, the sculptural boldness of Bilbao's Museo Guggenheim matches the quality of the art within.

tion, the **Museo de Bellas Artes** (Fine Arts Museum) is one of the country's very best collections. It offers a rich survey of Spanish classics — El Greco, Goya, and an honest "warts and all" portrait of Felipe IV by Velázquez — as well as Flemish and Italian masterpieces. The museum's upper floor is devoted to Basque and international 20th-century art.

CASTILLE AND LEÓN

This huge area north and west of Madrid is bordered by Portugal and the Costa Verde. An autonomous region with its capital at León, it consists of nine provinces — Ávila, Burgos, León, Palencia, Salamanca, Segovia, Soria, Valladolid and Zamora (Ávila and Segovia are covered in the **Around Madrid** section — see pages 37 and 43).

Burgos

Founded in A.D. 884 as a stronghold against the Moors, Burgos succumbed to the invaders but was reconquered in

951 and became the capital of Castile, an honor that it held until 1492 when the Catholic Monarchs transferred their court to Valladolid. In 1812 Burgos, then a French garrison during the Wars of Independence, was besieged by Wellington's troops. It was prominent, also, during the Spanish Civil War, when Franco was declared Head of State and Generalíssimo there in 1936. The city subsequently became the seat of the provisional government, and it was from La Isla Palace in Burgos, on April 1, 1939, that Franco proclaimed the cease-fire.

The city's most famous citizen, born in 1026, was Rodrigo Diaz — better known as the soldier of fortune, El Cid (see page 19), and his remains are interred in the **cathedral**, which is the third largest in Spain (after Sevilla and Toledo). This stunningly intricate Gothic jewel is also one of the most beautiful churches in the country. Construction began in 1221 but it took another 400 years to complete, and it holds attractions that are classical, historical and even eccentric. Don't miss the splendid **Constable's chapel** behind the altar,

Dressed in festive floral finery, Burgos cathedral is a Gothic jewel.

the burial place of Hernández de Velasco, Constable of Castile during the reign of the Catholic Monarchs. Gil de Siloé's altar of St Anne is partnered by his son Diego's exquisite golden stairway, built in 1519; it now leads nowhere and is only used during the highly ceremonious Easter celebrations. Look out, also, for the **Papamoscas** (Flycatcher), a clown dating from the 15th century, who sits above a clock high to the left of the main door, and opens and closes his mouth at each stroke of the bell.

Burgos is a charming city, and it's always fun to join the Burgalése on their evening stroll down the tree-lined Paseo del Espolón. This follows the banks of the normally placid Río Arlanzón, passing the decorative, crenellated **Arco de Santa María**, once the main entrance to the city. At the end of the Paseo, **El Cid** greets you, in the form of an impressive equestrian statue. Nearby, is the intricate and strange façade of the **Casa del Cordón** where, on April 23, 1497, Ferdinand and Isabella welcomed Columbus back from his second voyage to the New World. Back across the river, two noble Renaissance houses serve as the **Burgos Museum**.

On the western outskirts of Burgos, the **Convento de las Huelgas** was founded in the 12th century. Behind fortress-like walls, the complex is something of an architectural hybrid, with Romanesque elements and a superb Mudéjar-Gothic cloister. Kings were crowned and buried here, and a small museum displays some of the ecclesiastical treasures and artworks amassed by the convent's powerful abbesses.

León

León was founded in A.D. 68 by the Roman 7th legion, who built their fortifications on the hill where the cathedral now stands. During the sixth century the Romans were forced out by the Visigoths who, in turn, were defeated by the Moors early in the eighth century. Located on the edge of the Moors' scope of influence, control of the city fluctuated. By the 10th century it had been re-populated by Mozarabs (Christian refugees from the south) and, as the seat of the Kingdom of León, was considered the most important Christian city in Spain. However, in 996, the Moors invaded again and it wasn't until the 11th century that the city was finally reconquered. During the 12th century its prominence began to diminish until, in 1235, it amalgamated with Castile. León is a prosperous, modern city with a somewhat old-fashioned ambiance. Due to an isolated geographical location it does not receive too many tourists, but those who do make the effort to visit are amply rewarded.

León's most impressive monument is the 13th-century **Catedral de Santa María de Regla**. Clearly inspired by the Gothic cathedral at Chartres in France, it has the most glorious complement of stained glass in all of Spain — 125 huge windows and 57 smaller glassed areas dating from the 13th through to the 20th centuries. The west façade sports mismatched towers and elaborately carved portals. Tours of the cloister, an elegant mix of Gothic and Renaissance elements, lead to the **Diocesan Museum**, with archaeological exhibits and fine and applied arts.

A few streets west of the cathedral, an equestrian statue of St Isidro crowns the south side of the **Colegiata de San Isidro** (Collegiate Church). In the Moorish invasions, the saint's relics were evacuated to León from Sevilla, where he had been archbishop, and they still attract pilgrims to this day. The **San Isidro Museum** consists of the **Panteón Real** (Royal Pantheon), burial place of several kings and princes and home of magnificent frescoes, and the **Chapter Treasury Room**, which has notable exhibits.

The former **Monasterio de San Marco**, dating from the 16th century and built by Ferdinand and Isabella as a pilgrims' hospice, has a magnificent plateresque façade. Today, it doubles as one of Spain's finest *paradores*, with the **Museo Arqueológico Provincial** based in the cloister and sacristy.

☛ Salamanca

Hannibal made this his westernmost possession when he conquered this city in the third century B.C. Later, under the name of Helmántica, its strategic location helped it become an important city in the Roman Empire. In 1102,

León's parador once served as a hospice for pilgrims on the route to Compostela.

after periods of rule by the Visigoths and Moors, Salamanca was re-conquered by the forces of Alfonso VI. In 1218, Alfonso IX founded the first university in Spain, and it soon gained an international reputation. Between the 15th and early 18th centuries Salamanca was the main cultural center of the Spanish Empire. It suffered badly during the War of Independence, and it was entered by Wellington in the summer of 1812 just prior to the Battle of Salamanca. The cultural importance of Salamanca has been recognized by UNESCO, which has declared it to be a World Heritage Site.

The social hub of Salamanca is the graceful **Plaza Mayor**, considered to be the most perfect plaza in Spain, begun in 1729 during the reign of Felipe V. The street-level arcades, illuminated by delightful lanterns, support three additional stories and the most prominent buildings are the Town Hall and Royal Pavilion.

Salamanca has two connected, and very contrasting, cathedrals. The **Catedral Vieja** (Old Cathedral) was begun in 1114, finished a century later, and is one of the most important Romanesque structures in the country. Its most important work is the highly intricate 15th-century altar sculpted by the Italian, Nicolás Florentino. Look, also, for a retable featuring a fine 12th-century statue known as the *Virgen de la Vega* and the unusual Mudéjar dome in the **Capilla de Talavera**. Construction of the **Catedral Nueva** (New Cathedral) began in 1513 as the old one was too small, and although it has Renaissance and baroque additions, it is considered to be one of the last Gothic structures built in Spain. Inside, the triple-naved cathedral has marvelous baroque choir stalls and 18 side chapels, of which the most notable is the **Capilla Dorada** (Golden Chapel), with 110 sculptures. The **Diocesan Museum** in the old chapter house has a notable collection of paintings by Fernando Gallego, an underrated master of 15th-century Hispano-Flemish style.

Salamanca's **Universidad** (University), founded in 1218, was one of the greatest centers of learning in medieval Europe. The 16th-century plateresque façade of the main building is unbelievably intricate, and the lecture halls around the central patio illustrate centuries of architectural and decorative detail. Nearby, the **Patio de las Escuelas** is surrounded by plateresque buildings.

Salamanca has many other attractions, including numerous interesting convents, the **Salamanca Museum**, the circular Romanesque **Iglesia de San Marcos** (dating from 1178) and the very unusual **Casa de las Conchas** (House of Shells) built by a Knight of Santiago who decorated the exterior with hundreds of scallop-shell motifs (the symbol of St James of Compostela).

Around Salamanca

La Alberca, a modest rural town, is Old Spain personified. Heavily laden donkeys clatter down the main street; narrow alleys are lined by simple whitewashed homes, their delicate wooden balconies weighed down by flowerpots; and the Plaza Pública is put to use every year as a place to dry the bean harvest. The highlight of the local calendar is the Feast of the Assumption (August 15), when the entire population turns out to celebrate in traditional costume.

You can walk all the way around the hill town of **Ciudad Rodrigo** in no time. Just take the 2-km (1½-mile) path that follows the medieval defenses past the old castle (now a

Salamanca boasts two cathedrals, a university, a wealth of Renaissance palaces and Spain's most perfect plaza.

parador — see page 150). There are some dozen worthy old mansions in town, most with interesting stone carvings and inviting patios. The Plaza Mayor is distinguished by the **Casa Consistoral** (Town Hall), a 16th-century arcaded palace with a belfry, while the exterior of the **cathedral** is covered in fine sculptural details.

Soria

The smallest provincial capital of Spain, and the remotest in Castilla y León, spreads along a poplar-shaded bend of the Río Duero and typifies Old Castile. The small chapel of the **Ermita de la Soledad** contains a treasured 16th-century wooden statue of Christ. Across the street, the **Museo Numantino** (Museum of Numancia) specializes in relics found in the Roman ruins just north of town. Soria's collection of churches, all in toast-colored stone, is bountiful and beautiful, and almost all date from the 12th century. Among the most important are: **Santo Domingo,** with an expansive Romanesque façade; **San Juan de Rabanera,** with Byzantine touches and an early hint of Gothic; and the **Co-catedral de San Pedro,** with a plateresque portal and a Romanesque cloister. All but hidden on the left bank of the river, **San Juan de Duero** used to be a monastery of the Knights Templar. The remains of the original Romanesque **cloister** reveal finely carved capitals, and the church now serves as the medieval section of the Museo Numantino.

Valladolid

Valladolid may well be the least charming of the cities in this region, but it has more than its fair share of history and attractions. It was the home and birthplace of Castilian kings between the 12th and 17th centuries — including Felipe II

City of religious art and of elaborate façades, Valladolid once vied with Madrid for the title of capital of Spain.

and Felipe IV; capital of the empire during the reigns of Felipe II and Felipe III; the place where Ferdinand wed Isabella in 1469, thus marrying the kingdoms of Aragón, Catalonia, Naples, Castile, and León into a united Spain; home to Cervantes and Christopher Columbus; and, in 1809, headquarters for Napoleon.

Valladolid is one of the hotbeds of the Isabelline style — a form of overblown plateresque expressed in extravagant, florid ornamentation and named after Isabella of Castile. A perfect example of this style is the unusually elaborate façade of the **Colegio de San Gregorio**, founded in the late 15th century by Fray Alonso de Burgos, the Confessor to Isabella. The college has housed, since 1933, the **Museo Nacional de Escultura** (National Museum of Sculpture), the "Prado" of religious statuary, with works ranging from the 13th to the 18th centuries. The star here is the woodcarving genius of the Spanish Renaissance, Alonso Berruguete, said to have studied under Michelangelo.

The focal point for the entire city, and the surrounding area, is the massive statue of Christ that stands tall at its pinnacle atop the **cathedral**. Commissioned by Felipe II in the late 16th century, it was designed and started by Juan de Herrera, co-creator of Felipe II's Escorial complex, but completed much later, which accounts for its stylistic complexity. Juan de Juni, an Italian-trained Frenchman of the mid-16th century, created the altarpiece, and another of Juan de Arfe's monstrances, dating from 1587, can be seen in the museum.

On May 19, 1506 Christopher Columbus, then a broken man, died in the arcaded two-story **Casa-Museo de Colón** (House-Museum of Columbus), now restored to display relics and documents relating to the Age of Discovery. The **Casa de Cervantes** commemorates author Miguel Cervantes, creator of *Don Quixote*, who lived for several years in this ivy-covered house. The **Oriental Museum**, adjoining the massive edifice of the 18th-century **Royal College of the Agustinian Fathers**, has the best collection of its kind in Spain.

Around Valladolid

In Castile it is only natural to expect to see castles, and two of the best examples can be found close to Valladolid. **Coca Castle**, 63 km (39 miles) south of Valladolid is a late 15th-century masterpiece of Spanish Mudéjar military design, strongly influenced by Islamic architecture. And **Peñafiel Castle**, 35 km (22 miles) east of Valladolid is over 200 m (656 ft) long but less than 25 m (80 ft) across and sits stranded high on a lonely hilltop.

Hailed as Spain's prettiest fortress, 15th-century Coca Castle was the stronghold of the powerful Fonseca family.

Zamora

A strategic walled stronghold above the right bank of the Río Duero, the often besieged city of **Zamora** changed hands many times in the centuries of the Reconquest. To get the finest view of this appealing historic city, cross the Duero by the 14th-century bridge. From the south bank, you can admire the Byzantine cupola of the **cathedral**, built in the 12th century and roofed in curved stone tiles laid like fish scales. Its interior features a notable retable by Fernando Gallego, and there is a tapestry museum in the cloister.

Around Zamora

East of Zamora, the medieval hilltop town of **Toro** is a national monument. Besides some splendid Romanesque churches, convents, and mansions, and a ruined 10th-century castle, Toro's greatest pride is the **Iglesia Colegiata de Santa María la Mayor** (Collegiate Church of St Mary the Great). A Romanesque classic, it houses a most unusual 16th-century painting entitled *The Virgin and the Fly*, which is widely considered to be a faithful portrait of Isabella of Castile.

NAVARRA

Moving from west to east, the Pyrenees gain altitude, and the Basque character of the countryside and the people recedes. Navarra once extended into France, but the mountains now form a natural border between France and Spain. In fact, it is not a region that visitors frequent much, except at one time of the year, when they flock to **Pamplona** (Iruña) for the world-famous Fería de San Fermín (Feast of St Fermin), immortalized by Ernest Hemingway, which begins on July 7

Outside of festival time, Pamplona settles into its normal role as the quiet agricultural capital of Navarra.

The Running of the Bulls

Pamplona's Fiesta de San Fermín (Festival of St Fermin), specifically the **encierro** or "running of the bulls," so entranced the writer Ernest Hemingway that he immortalized it in his novel **The Sun Also Rises** (1926). Since his day, the fiesta has become an international crowd-puller, and the **encierro** is just part of the celebrations which run the gamut from wood-chopping contests to fireworks.

The **encierro** takes place daily from 7 to 12 July. At 8am when the bulls are released, serious corredores (runners), usually dressed in white with red sashes, attempt to run for a few steps, at least, side-by-side with the bulls along the route to the Plaza de Toros (bullring), while the main crowd are just happy to avoid the bulls if they can. Exciting it may be, but participants are regularly maimed and killed. Hemingway, known locally as Don Ernesto, is commemorated by a bust erected just outside the bullring.

every year. At that time the city is swamped with tens of thousands of people in festive mood. The early morning **encierros** (running of the bulls) that are a prelude to the afternoon **corridas** (bullfights) are most famous but, in fact, this fiesta has many other planned surprises — including a huge fireworks display every night – and many impromptu ones. For most people, the only practical way of seeing this famous event, however, is to book well in advance through a Basque Country travel specialist (a good starting point is the website <www.basquetravel.com>).

Visiting Pamplona at any other time of the year, you should visit the **cathedral**, with its magnificent cloister, and explore the narrow and colourful streets of the former Jewish quarter, south and west of the café-lined **Plaza del Castillo**.

LA RIOJA

Logroño

Logroño is the lively capital of Spain's premier wine region. Among medieval pilgrim travelers, the province of La Rioja was renowned for cheerful and attentive hospitality. Their first stop would have been **Santa María de Palacio**, dating from the 11th century and topped by a tall, graceful, pyramidal tower. The considerably younger **cathedral**, a few streets to the south of the church, features a generously sculpted main portal. Behind the cathedral lie the atmospheric narrow streets of the old town.

ARAGÓN

This ancient region consists of three provinces — Huesca, Zaragoza and Teruel — running from the Pyrenees on a north to south axis.

Huesca

The rugged northern section of this province is a sparsely populated and visually striking region that really is "undiscovered" Spain. The tallest peaks of all the Pyrenees belong to Aragón, and there are several good ski resorts in Astún, **Candanchú**, and **Formigal**.

Jaca, the gateway to the Aragón Pyrenees and an old stop on the Pilgrim Way, has been of great military significance for at least twelve centuries, ever since it figured in one of the earliest victories over the Moors. The enormous, low-lying 16th-century **fortress** at the edge of town is a symbol of its former strategic importance. Its other notable monument is its **cathedral**, which dates from the 11th century and is one of the oldest in Spain. Among the highlights are the fine Romanesque frescoes,

Renaissance sculptures and a plateresque altar retable.

Ordesa National Park, reckoned to be one of Europe's best-kept secrets, is a spectacular mountain park accessible from the village of Torla 60 km (37 miles) northeast of Jaca. Pyrenean chamois perch on the cliffs here, as do wild goats, roe deer, wild boar, and the last surviving herd of ibex (mountain goats with backward curving horns) in the Pyrenees. In the Ordesa Valley, dramatic canyon walls, 1,000 m (3,250 ft) in height, are cloaked in ancient beech, silver fir, and mountain pine forests. During summer the park can be busy, but snow prevents access from October to April.

Be prepared to walk if you want to see the spectacular canyons of the Ordesa National Park.

Zaragoza

Zaragoza, capital of Aragón and the region's one big town, can trace its origins back to the Iberians. In 19 B.C. the Romans founded the city of Caesaraugusta. Subsequently, the Moors held the city for 400 years until Alfonso I (The Fighter) reconquered it in 1118.

Zaragoza's Nuestra Señora Basilica stands on the spot where the Virgin appeared.

The long, narrow **Plaza del Pilar** is the social center of Zaragoza, and is home to magnificent monuments and modern fountains. Of the monuments, the cathedral-basilica of **Nuestra Señora del Pilar** (Our Lady of the Pillar), the largest and most important, is located in the center. According to tradition, the Virgin Mary appeared here in A.D. 40, standing on the jasper column that forms part of the elaborate **Capilla del Pilar**. The cathedral's superb main retable is the work of the sculptor Damián Forment. Zaragoza's other cathedral, **La Seo**, was built in the 12th century. Although the cathedral is mainly Gothic, it features Romanesque remnants, Mudéjar decorations, and striking baroque postscripts, plus a 17th-century belfry displaying one of the finest tapestry collections in Spain.

In 1988, workmen stumbled on the site of a **Roman Forum** built in the third century in front of the cathedral. Excavations have revealed the remains of a temple, homes, and shops, plus assorted statuary and general artifacts. Between the two cathedrals is **La Lonja**, considered the finest example of civil architecture in Zaragoza and constructed as an exchange between 1541 to 1551.

West of the city center, the beautifully restored Moorish **Aljafería Palace** was founded in the 11th century, then adapted by the Christian kings of Aragón after the Reconquest. Across the moat (now a sunken garden) you enter the world of Muslim Spain, something rarely seen this far north. The palace is now Aragón's parliament.

Teruel

The capital of Lower Aragón is a prime showcase for Mudéjar-style architecture. When Alfonso II of Aragón captured the town from the Moors in 1171, most Muslims chose to stay until their enforced expulsion at the end of the 15th century. This was time enough for the creation of lasting works of Mudéjar art.

The **cathedral's** Mudéjar elements include the finely decorated 13th-century brick tower and the lantern in the dome. Two other local towers are considered to be classics of the style: the **Torre San Martin** and **Torre del Salvador.**

Andorra: a tiny country in the Pyrenees

The tiny 487 sq km (188 sq mile) principality of Andorra is the world's only country whose official language is Catalan. After seven centuries of fiercely defended independence, it is now a cosmopolitan tax haven – especially for alcohol – regularly invaded by busloads of bargain hunters on a mission to plunder the bulging shops of Carrer Meritxell in Andorra-la-Vella, the capital. It is a shame that the principality's spectacular scenery takes second place to the shopping frenzy, for its verdant valleys backed by rugged mountains, country villages, and fine old Romanesque churches are a delight. Andorra also has well-equipped winter sports resorts.

The Gothic **Iglesia de San Pedro** (St Peter's Church) has a 13th-century Mudéjar tower. Adjoining the church is a chapel containing the mausoleum of the Lovers of Teruel, a star-crossed 13th-century couple whose tale of love lost and early death has inspired generations of Spanish writers.

CASTILLA-LA MANCHA

This is a geographically diverse area that wraps around Madrid to the east and south and consists of the provinces of Albacete, Ciudad Real, Cuenca, Guadalajara and Toledo (the latter is covered in **Around Madrid**.— see page 33).

La Mancha

The vast, parched plain of La Mancha, with its endless horizons and shimmering mirages, was the perfect setting for the adventures of author Miguel Cervantes' myopic, idealistic knight, Don Quixote, and his squire, Sancho Panza. Cervantes was born on the very edge of La Mancha, at Alcalá de Henares, in 1547. The son of an itinerant doctor, his education was minimal. Later, travels took him to Italy and then to Algeria as a prisoner of the Turks after the Battle of Lepanto (1571).

Back in Spain, it is said he wrote the first draft of *Don Quixote* in the prison of **Argamasilla de Alba** (northwest of Almagro). It was published in 1605 to great acclaim, and has been translated into more languages than any other book except the Bible. A sequel appeared in 1615, but a year later Cervantes was dead.

The names of several of La Mancha's villages and towns appear in the text of *Don Quixote*, none more important than **El Toboso** (in Toledo province), the home of Dulcinea, the woman of Quixote's dreams. Dulcinea's house is open to the public.

Albacete

This province does not have much of interest besides the windmills that dot the flat terrain.

Ciudad Real

Ciudad Real is, in truth, a distinctly underwhelming "Royal City." But the town of **Almagro** 25 km (16 miles) to the east has an impressive Plaza Mayor.

Cuenca

Cuenca, away from the main highways in the hill country of eastern Castilla-La Mancha, is not to be missed. The old town occupies a dramatic site perched on a precipice above the rivers Huécar and Júcar. It is here that Cuenca's famous

Cuenca's cliff-edge buildings rise dramatically from the limestone gorge carved by the rivers Huécar and Júcar.

medieval **Casas Colgadas** (Hanging Houses) literally hang out over the precipice void. The **Museo de Arte Abstracto Español** has a collection of outstanding contemporary Spanish paintings and sculptures, and the nearby **Museo de Cuenca**, a provincial archaeological museum, occupies a 14th-century palace. The **cathedral** is a unique 12th-century Gothic/Anglo-Norman structure that underwent significant renovations in the 17th century. Its interior is very plain but the treasures here include a 14th-century Byzantine diptych embellished with precious stones, unique in Spain.

Guadalajara

Sigüenza, northwest of the unexciting capital, Guadalajara, is home to a classic fortress, and an outsized **Plaza Mayor**, one of the most beautiful main squares in Spain. Founded by Visigoths and occupied by Moors, Sigüenza's **fort** was reconquered by Christian forces early in the 12th century. It became the headquarters of the bishops of Sigüenza, housing around 1,000 soldiers and more than 300 horses during the 15th century. Today, it is a *parador* (see page 150). At first sight, the crenellated **cathedral** also resembles a fortress. However, it contains a wealth of sculptural features, of which the most celebrated is the **sepulchre of "El Doncel"** ("The Page"). Commissioned by Queen Isabella, it honors a young servant killed fighting in Granada in 1486. Opposite, the **Museo Diocesano de Arte** packs its 14 halls with everything from prehistoric axes to an ethereal rendering of the Virgin by Zurbarán.

EXTREMADURA

Lying to the southwest of Madrid, Extremadura is bordered to the north by the province of Salamanca, to the east by the region of Castilla-La Mancha, to the west by Portugal and to the south by Andalucía. It consists of the two provinces of Cáceres and Badajoz, and is one of the least-visited regions of Spain. Extremadura reached a brief zenith during Roman times, when a provincial capital was established at Mérida, but its real fame comes from being the "Cradle of the Conquistadores," adventurers like Hernando Pizarro and Diego García, who colonized the Americas in the 16th century and brought back great riches to Spain.

Cáceres

Cáceres was founded in 34 B.C. by the Romans, who named it Norba Caesarina. Having declined after the Romans left, the Moorish invaders brought new prosperity during their nearly 400-year reign, calling it Hizn Quazri. Cáceres was finally reconquered by King Alfonso IX of León in 1229 and repopulated by families from León, Asturias, and Galicia who would later become the nobility of the region. The Order of Santiago, a brotherhood of knights, was founded here in the late 11th century. But it was not until the 16th century that the beautiful palaces and houses that give Cáceres its unique character were constructed.

The **Plaza Mayor** is the hub of local life, especially during the evening *paseo* when the historic buildings are illuminated, providing a dignified backdrop to the relaxed ritual. From there you can pass through the **Arco de la Estrella** (Star Arch) into the **Old Town** (Monumental Zone) and wander down a warren of streets lined with imposing buildings, sporting ostentatious heraldic shields, and often topped by huge storks' nests. The **Casa de las Veletas** (Weathervane House) has been turned into an excellent **provincial museum** featuring archaeological finds and displays of historical costumes and local customs, and has an old *ajibe* (Arabic reservoir) in the basement.

Guadalupe

The turrets, spires, and crenellations of the rambling **Monasterio de Nuestra Señora de Guadalupe** dominate **Guadalupe** from near and far. Surrounded by a huddle of small streets and squares the **monastery** — covering an area of about 2 hectares (5 acres) — is Spain's fourth most important pilgrimage site, and guardian of a precious wooden statue of the Virgin of Guadalupe, patron saint of the *conquistadores*. Founded in the 14th century, and enlarged four centuries later, the monastery is an architectural hybrid, with a flamboyant façade flanked by stern defensive towers, and with Mudéjar and Gothic cloisters. Guided tours (generally in Spanish) visit the cloisters, an embroidery museum, the chapter house, and the sacristy, which houses a remarkable collection of paintings by Zurbarán and others.

☛ Trujillo

Trujillo's hilltop skyline includes a heavily fortified **castillo**, which dominates the surrounding countryside, and the town is a worthy monument to its conquistador patrons. The eccentrically shaped **Plaza Mayor** is an interesting meeting-place of both distinguished and ordinary buildings. On the southwestern corner stands the **Palacio del Marqués de la Conquista**, which was built by a renowned local soldier, Hernando Pizarro. An equestrian statue of his half-brother, Francisco, stands on the square.

There are half a dozen other palaces around the town decorated with heroic portals, historic escutcheons, and pretty patios — all worthy of investigation. Storks' nests crown the clock tower over the Gothic church of **San Martin**, which has a long, dark nave paved with ancient tombstones. The Romanesque and Gothic church of **Santa**

María la Mayor boasts a fine retable in Hispano-Flemish style. Two imposing stone seats on the balcony were built for the Catholic Monarchs, Ferdinand and Isabella.

Alcántara

In its day, the magnificent six-arched **Roman bridge** over the Tagus near **Alcántara** was a renowned engineering feat. No less than 194 m (636 ft) long, with extraordinarily high arches, it is altogether so impressive that the town was named after it: in Arabic *al-Qantara* means "the bridge." Built entirely without mortar, the bridge has stood since its completion in 105 A.D.

Conquistador and Trujillo native, Francisco Pizarro.

Badajoz

The gateway to Portugal, **Badajoz** is the biggest city in Extremadura. The medieval walled city is entered through the **Puerta de Palmas** — an ancient fortified city gate. Another arch used to bar the way to the **citadel** overlooking the Guadiana river, where the rulers of the Moorish kingdom of Badajoz held sway. The **cathedral**, founded in the 13th century, with its heavy walls and pinnacled tower, is largely Gothic but with Renaissance additions. Inside are impressive choir stalls, paintings, tapestries, and tombstones. The **Museo Provincial de Bellas Artes**, which exhibits some good Flemish tapestries, is on the same square.

Around Badajoz

At the end of the Cantabrian Wars, Caesar Augustus chose to settle veteran legionnaires in the province of Lusitania. And in 25 B.C., Augusta Emerita was chosen to house veterans of the 5th and 10th legions. Not long after, it was designated as capital for the province and it soon grew to be the most important city in the Iberian Peninsula, and one of the most important in the Roman Empire. Today **Mérida**, a sleepy modern town and capital of Extremadura, can lay claim to the greatest number of Roman remains in any Spanish town.

The *pièce de résistance* is the partially restored first-century B.C. **Teatro Romano** with seating for more than 5,500 spectators where, in summer, Greek and Roman plays are produced. The elliptical **Anfiteatro** next door (also known as the Circus Maximus) was designed to hold 15,000 spectators for gladiatorial contests and chariot

Sons of Trujillo

Of all the conquistador towns, none is more proud of its sons' exploits than Trujillo. The most famous were the Pizarros, who conquered Peru, but other natives were Diego García Paredes and Francisco de las Casas, who both founded towns called Trujillo in Venezuela and Honduras respectively, and Francis Orellana, the first European navigator of the Amazon.

Diego García in particular had a fearsome reputation. He was known as the Extremadura Samson and among his legendary feats of strength he is said to have picked up the font in Santa María la Mayor to carry holy water to his mother. The tombs of the Pizarros and that of García can be seen in the same church.

Mock naval battles were staged in Mérida's Roman amphitheatre by flooding the arena.

races. At times it was even flooded to host re-creations of great naval battles.

Almost next door is the award-winning **Museo Nacional de Arte Romano**. Its beautifully displayed collections include examples of Roman statuary, locally minted coins, and paintings discovered on the podium of the arena. Around town are many other Roman monuments: a temple to Diana, an aqueduct, and a 0.8-km (½-mile) bridge spanning the Guadiana.

Zafra is the most attractive of southern Extremadura's towns, and is often referred to as **Sevilla la Chica** (Little Sevilla). Its charming white houses converge on two arcaded plazas – Plaza Grande and Plaza Chica – recalling its Moorish origins. The medieval Alcázar, now a sumptuous *parador* (see page 150), was where adventurer Hernán Cortés stayed before setting off to conquer Mexico.

THE BALEARIC ISLANDS

In the western Mediterranean, the Balearics comprise a sunny cross-section of landscapes from mountainous Mallorca to the flat Formentera.

☞ ## Mallorca

For decades Mallorca (Majorca as it is known by some in the English-speaking world) has been Europe's playground. The island measures 72 km (45 miles) by 96 km (60 miles), and well over half of the population lives in the animated and cosmopolitan capital city of **Palma de Mallorca. La Seu**, the formidable Gothic cathedral, was founded in 1299 — after the Reconquest by Jaime I (the Conqueror) — and totally dominates the seafront. The interior's magnificent proportions and traditional splendor are enhanced by Gaudi's *baldachin* hanging over the main altar.

Alongside is the classical-style **Palacio Almudaina**, with delicately arched and covered balconies. This was once a palace for the Muslim governors. After the Reconquest, it was renovated for the medieval kings of Mallorca and it now houses the National Heritage Museum in one wing.

High on the hill overlooking, and commanding the land and sea approaches to, Palma is the distinctive cylindrical silhouette of the tower of the 14th-century **Castillo de Bellver**.

Exploring Mallorca's 965-km (600-mile) long coastline clockwise from Palma, the first stop must be the new marina and restaurant complex of **Portals Nous**, where the size of the yachts are sure to impress. High-rise **Magaluf**, though, is impressive mainly to the Brits that flock there in tens-of-thousands. **Port d'Andratx** lies close to the western tip of the island, on a sheltered bay popular with boating fans. **Banyalbufar**, to the north, has some of the island's finest terraced orchards, built in tiers, and **Esporlas** has the **La Granja**, a cross between a stately home, craft center, traditional farmhouse, and museum of rural life.

Valldemosa, which lies just inland, is a magnet for tourists who come to visit the monastery of **Sa Cartuja**, built on top of a royal castle. Here you can see exhibits relating to the novelist Georges Sand and her companion, Frédéric Chopin, who rented some rooms here between 1838 and 1839

Turning back to the coast road, which in itself is a challenge, the next stop is **Deía**, probably the island's most attractive town, a pretty hilltop

Statues and niches decorate Palma de Mallorca's elegant waterfront cathedral.

community built from honey-colored stone. Something of an artists' colony — the grave of Robert Graves, the British author of *I Claudius* lies in the cemetery — this is also a good base for visiting the **Tranmuntana** region in the northwest. A favorite haunt of the independent traveler, there are few beaches here, but a spectacular — and hair-raising — road allows fantastic views.

Cala en Turqueta, a glorious beach in the southwest of Menorca.

The town of **Sóller** is linked to Palma by a delightful narrow-gauge railway, whose polished wood carriages make the hour-long journey through orchards and then mountain scenery. An old San Francisco-style open tram then travels the short journey down to the seaside and the pretty harbor of **Port de Sóller**.

The road between **Sóller** and **Pollenca** is difficult and not particularly interesting with the exception of the **Monastery of Lluc**, home to *La Moreneta* (the Black Lady). **Pollenca** itself is worth a visit to see the *Calvario* and a Roman bridge, whilst the nearby **Port de Pollenca** is a very pleasant resort, not spoilt too much by tourism. To the north are the isolated and splendid cliffs of the **Cabo de Formentor**. Carrying on south, you will find the walled town of **Alcudia** with its Roman ruins and popular Sunday market, and the busy beach resort of the **Port de D'Alcudia**.

The main town at the easternmost end of the island is **Cala Ratjada**, a combined port and resort. **Porto Cristo**, further south, is a pleasant resort built around a protected harbor. One of the most popular tourist excursions on Mallorca, however, is a trip to the nearby **Cuevas del**

Drach (Dragon's Caves), where you can see dramatically lit formations, and the similar **Cuevas de Artá**.

There are several other small towns around the lower east and southern coastlines, but none of any consequence until you arrive at **El Arenal** and the other resorts that combine to make the **Bay of Palma** the busiest area on Mallorca.

Menorca

Menorca, the second largest of the Balearic islands, is one-fifth the area of Mallorca, and receives a much smaller number of visitors. It is a very pleasant, green, and undulating island dotted with coastal towns and resorts as well as many scenic beaches and coves — some of which can only be reached on foot or by four-wheel-drive vehicle.

The capital and deep-water harbor of **Mahón** (Maó in Menorquí, the local language) was occupied by the British for a large part of the 18th century. The little city clusters on the cliffs above the port, and buildings in the older quarter of town have a distinctly Georgian appearance. A boat trip around the harbor makes a fun excursion.

Ciudadela (Ciutadella), on the west coast, also has a fine harbor, but is more akin to Andalucía than old England. **Ses Arcades**, the street leading to the Gothic cathedral built in the 14th century, is all archways and completely Moorish. Visit the **city museum** in the Town Hall (Ayuntamiento) for its rather curious exhibits of island history.

The best beach and resort on the island is **Cala Santa Galdana**, a beautiful horseshoe-shaped cove developed in a restrained fashion. Further along the coast, on the way to Maó, is the **Cova d'en Xoroi**, and it shouldn't be missed. Here caves in the tall cliffs have been made into an innovative bar with fantastic views. **Fornells**, on the north coast, is another relaxed resort and still an active fishing port.

Ibiza (Eivissa)

Besides those simply seeking some sun and sea Ibiza, these days, caters to the seriously hip, from assorted rock stars and artists to dance-crazy youths, and offers accommodation, restaurants, shops and entertainment accordingly.

Ibiza Town (Eivissa), the island's capital, is dominated by its old town, **Dalt Vila**, whose encircling walls are the longest in Spain. Within the walls you will find a cobbled maze packed with whitewashed houses, tiny bars, shops, flea markets, and restaurants serving local fare. The capital has two **archaeological museums** boasting a treasury of Carthaginian art. One, the **Puig des Molins**, is built adjacent to a necropolis, and tours are given of the burial chambers.

It is the beaches, though, that most people come for. They start immediately south of town, but the best, and certainly the trendiest, are generally agreed to be those at **Las Salinas.**

Bougainvillea thrives in the hot summer climate of Ibiza, noted as much for its wildflowers as its wild party scene.

Santa Eularia, to the north, is an important resort as is **Sant Antoni** on the west coast, though this is very much the land of the cheap package hlioday. **Portinatx** and **San Miguel**, in the north, are much smaller and quieter resorts, and you can visit caves at San Miguel.

The bright lights, loud music, exotic dress codes and, it must be said, the easy availability of drugs attract young people from all over northern Europe to Ibiza. The clubs to which they are attracted are found, mainly, in the south of the island. Typical of these is **Privilege** which, at 7,000 sq m (1.73 acres) has a capacity of 10,000 people, and advertises itself as the largest dance club in the world.

Formentera

The 11-km (7-mile) sea voyage from Ibiza takes 75 minutes by boat, or around half that by hydrofoil but, whichever you choose, it's more often than not a rough passage. There is no airport here, and very little water, which has hindered large-scale development.

Once the sole retreat of the backpacker and laid-back beach bum, Formentera now caters to package tourists who come for the extensive, unspoiled beaches. There is not much to do here besides sunbathing — mostly in the nude — and windsurfing.

THE CANARY ISLANDS

The seven volcanic islands that form the Canaries in the Atlantic, just off the coast of North Africa, are as different from each other as can possibly be and provide a semi-tropical escape for those in search of winter sun.

The Canaries are split into two provinces: that of Santa Cruz de Tenerife consists of the westernmost islands of Tenerife, El Hierro, La Gomera and La Palma, while the eastern province of Las Palmas de Gran Canaria consists of Gran Canaria, Lanzarote and Fuerteventura. All the islands are different from each other and appeal to differing tastes — some better for walking, others for beach holidays..

Tenerife

The largest of the Canaries, Tenerife offers more attractions and more contrasts than any of its island neighbors. **Santa Cruz de Tenerife**, in the northeast, is the capital and administrative center of the westerly Canaries. In reality, though, it doesn't hold much appeal for tourists. By contrast, **Puerto de la Cruz**, on the attractive north coast is a popular resort, despite not having a beach. This deficiency has been overcome by the genius of the late César Manrique who designed **Lago Martiánez**, a 3-hectare (8-acre) complex of tropical lagoons, cascading fountains and sunbathing terraces cleverly landscaped with lush palms and black and white volcanic rocks to blend perfectly into the seafront.

The **Loro Parque** should not be missed, and is a delight for all ages. It has the world's largest collection of parrots — more than 300 species and subspecies. It is also home to an eclectic array of animals, including gorillas, chimpanzees, tigers, jaguars, alligators, sea-lions, dolphins and numerous other creatures that are exhibited in carefully, and creatively, designed spaces. Look, also, for the underwater world of the aquarium and shark tunnel, and the newest, and undoubtedly most inventive, display — Planet Penguin, the largest Penguinarium in the world.

Jardín Botánico, founded by royal decree in 1788, and located on the road to Orotava, is the oldest local attraction. On the same road, **Banañera El Guanche** is a working banana plantation with a great collection of exotic flowers, trees, shrubs, and cacti.

The highlight of the island in every sense, **Mount Teide** is a volcanic cone in the Las Cañadas del Teide National Park, and Spain's highest mountain at 3,717 m (12,200 ft). Particularly beautiful in May and June when the wildflowers are in bloom, the park's spectacular scenery makes for great hiking. It is strange in mid-winter to see this gigantic snow-capped peak dominating beaches full of sun bathers and swimmers. The visitor center has details of walking trails and guided walks. You can also get to within 163 m (535 ft) of the summit by cable car (*teleférico*), though you need to arrive early to avoid queues.

Often capped with snow, Tenerife's Mount Teide is Spain's highest peak.

El Hierro

Until the voyages of Columbus, El Hierro was considered the end of the world. Even now, it attracts few visitors except keen walkers, and tourist facilities are limited. **Valverde** is the tiny, quiet capital.

La Gomera

La Gomera remains an unspoiled island of steep, green ter-raced hills and tranquil valleys. Boats and hydrofoils make the short trip from Tenerife dock and at **San Sebastián,** the main town, notable for its connections with Christopher Columbus, including a local church where he prayed and the house where he supposedly stayed in 1492. A delight for walkers, the **Garajonay National Park** is a World Heritage Site and home to the Alto de Garajonay, Gomera's highest peak — 1,487 m (4,878 ft). The island's one and only beach resort is in the south, at the low-key **Playa de Santiago**.

La Palma

The most northwesterly of the Canaries, La Palma is lush and green. Santa Cruz de la Palma, the capital, is an appealing small town. The main attraction here is the magnificent **Caldera de Taburiente**, a giant crater that has a circumference of some 27 km (17 miles) and which drops around 700 m (2,300 ft) into a fertile valley. The island is perfect walking country, with marvelous views. The world-renowned Palma observatory, only open to the public a few days each summer, is on top of the **Roque de los Muchachos**, the highest peak in Palma 2,423 m (7,950 ft).

Gran Canaria

Almost circular in shape, Gran Canaria has been described as a continent in miniature. The coastline ranges from awesome cliffs to golden dunes; inland, you can choose between stark mountains and tranquil valleys. It is also well supplied with beaches, shopping centers, and sophisticated nightlife.

Las Palmas, capital of the island and province, is a major commercial center, cosmopolitan resort, and seaport all in one. The **Playa de las Canteras**, its famous sandy beach in the heart of the city, is 3 km (2 mile) long and is protected by an offshore reef. The **Santa Catalina Park** is one gigantic outdoor café that buzzes night and day.

The main beach resorts are on the island's south coast. **Playa del Inglés** is a large, crowded and spread-out package-tour center. **Maspalomas** is famous for its dunes, which are sufficiently large and unspoiled to constitute a mini-Sahara, and is known as an unofficial nudist beach, while **San Agustin** is quiet and tidy. West of **Maspalomas**, **Puerto Rico** and **Puerto de Mogán** offer differing charms.

Cruz de Tejeda, at 1,463 m (4,800 ft), is a popular vantage point in the center of the island, and the panorama includes two distinctive rock formations that were once worshipped by the Guanches — the original inhabitants of the Canaries who migrated from North Africa.

Lanzarote

Lanzarote is a startling place, representing the triumph of civilization over a hostile environment. Declared a Biosphere Reserve by UNESCO, the island is pock-marked with over 300 volcanoes. The locals grow onions, tomatoes, potatoes, melons, and grapes, which spring in abundance from the volcanic ash. It was the birthplace of César Manrique whose eclectic sculptures and architectural creations undoubtedly enhance the island.

Arrecife is the undistinguished capital. The island's main resort, **Puerto del Carmen**, lies to the south and

Prickly pears flourish in Lanzarote's surprisingly fertile black volcanic soil.

has a long, golden beach, while **Costa Teguise**, just to the north of Arrecife, offers more upmarket facilities.

The highlight of a trip to Lanzarote is a visit to the ☛ **Montañas de Fuego** ("Mountains of Fire") in the Timanfaya National Park. The stark but scenically magnificent park starts just north of Yaiza. Its bizarre landscape of lava flows and rust-red mountains was largely formed over 16 months of cataclysmic volcanic activity during 1730–1731. There is an information center and parking lot at Islote de Hilario, from where bus tours depart to explore the incredible lunar landscape.

César Manrique's magical creativity can be seen at the **Fundación César Manrique** art gallery, the prickly **Jardín de Cactus**, the caves of **Jameos del Agua**, the sculpture of the **Monumento al Campesino** and the **Mirador del Río**, which offers absolutely spectacular views.

Fuerteventura

Situated less than 100 km (60 miles) off the coast of North Africa, and just south of Lanzarote, Fuerteventura is a beach bum's paradise, courtesy of the Sahara. There are miles of golden sandy beach, and the winds that originally blew the sand here still ensure superb windsurfing, for which the Playa de Sotavento is world-famous. At the southern tip of the island, the **Jandía peninsula** offers terrific beaches, the best of which are on the less-developed **Costa Calma**. Besides watersports there is little else to do on this arid, tree-less island. **Betancuria**, is an isolated attractive inland oasis. It was Fuerteventura's first capital, and boasts the splendid 17th-century church of **Santa Maria**.

Betancuria, the ancient capital of Fuerteventura, was founded well inland to escape pirate attacks.

WHAT TO DO

As well as its historical attractions, Spain is blessed with marvelous beaches and an incredibly varied coastline. Some of Spain's resorts are very popular and crowded in the main season, but even the famous Costa del Sol still has relatively wild and undeveloped areas, and those seeking quieter resorts do not have to look very far to find them.

WATERSPORTS

Water-skiing. Water-skiing is available at large resorts — as are jet-skiing and parasailing. The Balearics and east-coast resorts at La Manga, Costa Dorada, and Costa Brava are all good places to try this exhilarating sport.

Windsurfing. This is a hugely popular sport. Tuition, equipment, and wetsuit rental are available at many resorts. Advanced windsurfers should go to Tarifa in southern Spain (see page 80) or Jandía peninsula on Fuerteventura (one of the Canary Islands). **Scuba diving.** There is good diving off the Costa Brava, Costa de Almería, Costa Tropical and the Canary and Balearic

Lilos in the style of Salvador Dalí for sale on the Costa Dorada.

Islands. Local dive operators can arrange tuition, permits, and equipment rental.

Boating. Most tourist beaches have a variety of craft for rent — light catamarans are very popular. Sailing is particularly good off the Costa Brava, the Balearic and Canary Islands, in the Bay of Cádiz, and at Santander and Laredo on Spain's north coast.

LAND SPORTS

Golf. Spain is world-famous for golf, with over 100 courses on the mainland and islands. Not every pro is a Sevvy Ballesteros, but the quality of instruction is generally high. The greatest concentration of courses is on the Costa del Sol, where road signs declare this also to be the Costa del Golf. On the east coast, the Valencian courses of El Saler and El Escorpian are highly rated and of good value; the La Manga Club on the Costa Cálida has three championship courses.

Jai-Alai — The World's Fastest Ball Game

The ancient Basque game of *jai-alai* (pronounced "high-a-lie," but sometimes also known as *pelota*) is played throughout the Basque region. Every town and almost every village, no matter how tiny, has a *frontón*, or pitch, rather like a squash court, where the players hurl themselves around after the *pelota* (ball), which is propelled at the back wall at speeds of up to 303 km/h (188 mph) by woven straw scoops attached to the players' hands.

The basic rules are similar to tennis or squash — the ball may only bounce once on the ground; each game comprises 7 to 9 points. Far more complex is the betting, which is largely incomprehensible to outsiders.

Of the islands, Mallorca has a number of fine courses, while Gran Canaria boasts Spain's oldest golf club, in a stunning setting. For an overview of what's available, request a golfing map of Spain from the national tourist office.

Tennis. Tennis is popular in Spain and many hotels and villa complexes have their own tennis courts — some even have a resident professional. The Costa del Sol is probably the biggest center for tennis tuition and the east coast La Manga Club is one of the best tennis centers in Europe.

Horseback-riding. There are ranches and equestrian centers all over Spain. Many offer instruction and a range of outings on horseback from a stimulating cross-country excursion or an overnight trek. A favorite place for this sport is the Alpujarra region, south of the Sierra Nevada.

Skiing. Spain has many ski resorts that are attracting an increasing number of devotees. The Sierra Nevada resort of Solynieve, just outside Granada, may be the most famous, but there are many other places across the Pyrenees range (including Andorra) and more in the Picos de Europa.

Walking, hiking, and climbing. Spain offers numerous opportunities for walking along the network of national and regional footpaths, many of which pass through national parks and nature reserves. National, regional and local tourist offices can supply further information.

SHOPPING

Modern Spain has long since shed its image as the bargain basement of Europe. However, fans of the truly kitsch should have no fear, for among the genuinely tasteful souvenirs of a Spanish vacation — ceramics, leather goods, food treats from olive oil to nougat — the straw donkey and bullfight poster are still alive and kicking.

For a quick survey of what Spaniards are buying, browse through the big department stores, especially the ubiquitous El Corte Inglés. There are branches in most towns, and unlike the majority of Spanish businesses they stay open through the lunch-and-siesta break until about 9:00pm in the evening.

For quality crafts, more than a dozen cities have branches of Artespaña, the official showcase for items created by Spanish artisans.

Here are a few suggestions for best buys in Spain:

Antiques. You will find few bargains in genuine antiques shops or stalls. However, almost every Spanish town has an open-air *rastro* on Sunday mornings — those in Madrid and Sevilla are attractions in their own right — and provide plenty of fun for browsers.

Artificial pearls. Made in Mallorca, these are so convincing that experts are often fooled. Some say the test is to rub them along your teeth — the real ones are rougher.

Ceramics. Each region has its own distinctive designs and color schemes. Hand-painted *azulejos* (tiles of Moorish origins) are also popular and collectable. Talavera de la Reina, west of Madrid, is a major center for top-rated ceramics.

Buy a fan to flutter and stay cool the romantic way.

Damascene and Toledo steel. This is a specialty of Toledo, though the art of damascening (inlaying the steel with intricate gold designs) originated in Damascus.

Embroidery and lace. Pretty embroidered linen and traditional lacework is sold all over Spain. Look for lace *mantillas,* those lightweight shawls used for covering the shoulders. Be wary of gypsy street sellers offering bargain prices; their goods are generally of much poorer quality and made anywhere but in Spain.

Glassware. Mallorca is the center for glassmaking. The typical blue, green, or amber bowls, glasses, and pitchers are sold in many mainland stores.

Leather. Top-quality Spanish leather products range from sturdy belts, wallets, and riding boots to elegant handbags and jackets. Beware of the less expensive bags and belts on sale at stalls and markets; more often than not these are imported from Morocco and you will pay two to three times the original price.

Valencian porcelain. Lladró figurine collectors can stock up at stores all over Spain; less detailed models from the same workshop go under the name of Nao porcelain.

ENTERTAINMENT

Since Spaniards don't start thinking about their dinner until 9:00 or 10:00pm, Spanish nightlife tends to keep going far later than in other countries. After a leisurely meal, it's on to the music bar (occasionally live music, but generally a video screen pumping up the volume) for a drink and a chance to catch the latest football score before deciding where to go next. Only then will they actually hit the disco or nightclub — around 2:00am. Barcelona is one of the most fashionable nightspots in Europe. Madrid is the city that never sleeps, and Ibiza is the leader of Europe's clubbing scene.

Folklore and Festivals

The best way to experience Spanish customs is to experience a local *fería* (festival). Every community, no matter its size, has its own fería — with the larger towns and cities often celebrating two. Check with the tourist office for details of local celebrations during your stay. Here's a selection of the very best from around the country:

February/March: Carnival. Processions in Santa Cruz de Tenerife, Cádiz, and Sitges.

March/April: Semana Santa (Holy Week). Processions in all major cities from Palm Sunday until Easter Sunday, with the most famous in Sevilla.

April: April Fair. Parades, dancing, and bullfights in Sevilla.

May: Festival of the Patios in Córdoba and International Horse Fair in Jerez de la Frontera.

May/June: Fiesta de San Isidro. Bullfighting, concerts, and fun fairs in Madrid.

June: Corpus Christi. Festivities in Granada, Toledo, Sitges, and the Canary Islands.

July: Fiesta de San Fermín. Bullruns, bullfights, and festivities in Pamplona. Music Festival, Granada. Festival of St. James, Santiago de Compostela.

August: Assumption. National holiday on August 15th with numerous towns holding festivals. Traditional commemoration in La Alberca (Salamanca). Summer Fair, Málaga.

September: Logroño Wine Harvest, wine festival in Jerez de la Frontera. Mercé Feria de San Miguel, Torremolinos. Meced Festival, music and folklore in Barcelona.

October: Pilar Festival. Processions, bullfights and folklore in Zaragoza.

Flamenco

Throbbing guitars, snapping fingers, stamping heels, colorful dresses and soul-stirring songs lure local enthusiasts and visitors to Spain's flamenco nightclubs. There are two main groups of songs: the bouncier, more cheerful type is known as *cante chico*; the *cante jonto* deals with love, death, and human drama in slow, piercing style. Unfortunately, most people will only get to see the show-biz style *tablaos flamenco*, for which their hotel gets a percentage for every ticket sold. For the real thing, you have to head for the specialist bars and clubs of Andalucía, the home of flamenco, and it's best to ask a taxi driver to take you to them as the performers often move from one to another without much notice. In Madrid, the **Corral de la Moreira** — though not inexpensive — offers a fascinating glimpse into the flamenco world.

Cultural Activities

Spaniards take **opera** very seriously, along with their home grown stars Plácido Domingo, José Carreras, Teresa Berganza, and Monserrat Caballé. There are three great venues: Barcelona's Gran Teatre del Liceu, Madrid's Teatro Real and Sevilla's Teatro de la Maestranza.

Distinctive, timeless, and passionate, flamenco is music to stir the depths of the soul.

For **concerts**, Madrid's Auditorio Nacional de Música, inaugurated in 1988, is home to the Spanish National Orchestra. Check with local tourist offices for details of concerts and recitals in other cities. They often take place in historic surroundings such as churches and palaces.

For **drama**, Spanish as well as foreign plays — classical and contemporary — can be seen in theaters all over the country.

Foreign films are generally dubbed before they are shown in a Spanish **cinema**, but in major cities and some resorts, cinemas may show films in their original version (labeled "v.o.") with Spanish subtitles.

CHILDREN

Long, sunny days and soft, sandy beaches mean that coastal Spain is a favorite family destination. Many hotels have special features for junior guests, ranging from organized poolside games and outings to babysitting facilities. When seawater and sandcastles start to wear thin, you can try some of the following:

Make a splash. Water parks are a highly popular alternaselves down waterslides and ride the machine-made waves, the less active types can top off their tans in landscaped gardens. Additional attractions often include ten-pin bowling and mini-golf.

Go-karting. A favorite with the kids (not to mention their parents), go-kart tracks are common along the *costas* and in the Canary Islands.

A night out. The Spanish take their kids out at night, so why not do likewise? Older children will probably enjoy a colorful flamenco show, and there are no restrictions on children accompanying adults into bars, restaurants, or cafés.

Fiesta. Older children will love the firework displays and music, while the younger kids watch the dancers and giant *papier-mâché* figures wide-eyed. Carnival is always a colorful event where the local children usually wear the best costumes. There is nothing to stop you from also dressing up and joining in. It's great fun and you're sure to be welcome.

The fun of the fair. Most big towns or resorts have a *parque de atracciones* where the rides range from the old-fashioned carousel and big wheel to high-tech thrills. Barcelona's two fun fairs, at Montjuïc and Tibidabo, deserve a special mention for their first-class rides and tremendous views.

Animal life. The Barcelona Zoo, with its famous albino gorilla and a killer whale and dolphin show, is acclaimed as one of the finest zoo parks in Europe. Elsewhere on the coast and on the islands, marine parks with performing dolphins, sea lions, and other animal shows are becoming increasingly popular.

Budding rally stars hone their skills on the go-kart track.

Bullfighting

Like it or loathe it, it is impossible to escape the impact that the *corrida* (bullfight) has on Spanish life. The colorful *carteles* (posters) that advertise these events are ubiquitous in Spain and the *temporada* (season) lasts from March to October. The bullfight isn't considered a sport — a contest between two equals. Instead it is a highly ritualistic event in which man pits his intelligence against a magnificent and powerful animal.

The corrida consists of three *tercios* (acts), each with its own rituals, though the volatile nature of the contest dictates that no one knows exactly what is going to happen in each. In the first tercio, the *toro bravo* (wild bull) is released and the matador (literally "killer") takes stock of the bull making passes with his large magenta and yellow *capote* (cape). Next the *picadores* — mounted men armed with wooden poles tipped with a *puya*, a pointed metal head — attempt to lance the bull behind its *morillo* (large neck muscle), causing the bull's head to lower.

In the second tercio, the *banderilleros*, part of the matador's *cuadrilla* (team of assistants) work on foot to plant long sticks with a barbed end and covered with colored paper into the bull's back.

The third and final tercio, the *faena*, sees the matador return, without his *montera* (hat) and armed with just the much smaller, dark red *muleta* (cape). This is what he gets paid handsomely for. For the next 13-minutes — legally it cannot last any longer, and often it is shorter — he adjusts his skills to the characteristics and strength of the bull, with intricate passes that bring man and bull into close harmony. If all is going well, the band will strike up an accompanying *pasodoble*; but, when the matador is ready for the "moment of truth", the most dangerous point in the corrida, the band will unceremoniously stop.

It is then that the matador, muleta in his left hand directing the bull's attention away from his body and sword in his right, will spin over the dangerous right horn, trying to deliver an *espada* (sword) stroke between the shoulder blades and into the heart, with the aim of killing the bull instantly.

EATING OUT

The Spanish take their food very seriously and you will rarely be disappointed by the variety and flavor of the hearty portions served in local **restaurantes** (restaurants) throughout Spain. Each region has its own distinctive culinary strengths, from the seafood creations of the north to the rice platters of the east, from the roasts of the central area to the succulent hams and fried fish of the south. And for every dish, there is usually a locally grown wine to match.

WHERE TO EAT

Spanish restaurants are graded by the **Tenedor(es)** (fork) system. One fork is the lowest grade, five forks is the élite. These ratings, however, are awarded according to the facilities and degree of luxury that the restaurant can offer, not for the quality of the food. (See Recommended Restaurants page 182.)

Almost all Spanish restaurants offer a good value *menú del día* (daily special). This is normally a three-course meal, including house wine, at a very reasonable set price.

The prices on the menu include a service charge and taxes, but it is customary to leave a tip of 5 to 10 percent if you have been served efficiently. Bars and cafés, like restaurants, usually include a service charge, but additional small tips are customary. Prices are slightly lower if you stand or sit at the bar rather than occupy a table.

Two notes of caution: the prices of *tapas*, those tasty bar snacks, are not always indicated and can be surprisingly expensive: it is not unusual for the cost of several tapas to equate to the price of the *menú del día* at an inexpensive bar/restaurant. Also, ask how much your meal will cost when ordering fish or seafood, which is priced by the 100g weight. The price is based on the uncooked weight and can be more than you expected.

Meal times are generally later in Spain than in some parts of Europe. The peak hours are from 1:00 to 3:30pm for lunch and from 8:30 to 11:00pm for dinner. In Madrid and the south, meals are eaten very late, only starting at around 10:00pm. However, in tourist areas or big cities, you can get a meal at most places just about any time of day.

WHAT TO EAT

Breakfast

For Spaniards, this is the least significant meal of the day and will probably just consist of *tostada* (toast) or a roll and coffee. If you have a sweet tooth, *churros* are deep-fried sugared doughnut-like temptations, made for dipping into your coffee. To make guests feel at home, most hotels offer breakfast buffets with a selection of cereals, fresh and dried fruit, cold meats, and cheeses, plus bacon and eggs.

Lunch and Dinner

The classic Spanish dish is *paella*, named after the black iron pan in which saffron-flavored rice is cooked in stock. The chef then adds various combinations of squid, *chorizo* (spicy sausage), chicken, mussels, prawns, rabbit, onions, peppers, peas, and so on, according

The classic Spanish snack: air-cured ham from the mountains.

Synonymous with Spain: a paella of rice, shrimps, squid, and peas.

to the type of *paella* advertised on the menu. It is always cooked to order (usually for a minimum of two people) and outside of tourist areas is normally only served at lunch.

There are two other national favorites well known to visitors. The first is *gazpacho*, a delicious Andalucían chilled soup made with chopped tomatoes, peppers, cucumbers, onions, and fried croutons. The second is *tortilla*, or potato omelette. There are many variations on this theme, served hot or cold.

Regional Tastes

Every province — and almost every town — in Spain seems to have its own locally produced sausage, cheese, or *paella* variation, and their own secret ingredients for *cocido*, a rich cold-weather meat and vegetable hot-pot. Here are a few suggestions for what's cooking around the country, moving roughly north to south.

Galicia: Famed for great seafood, particularly *pulpo* (octopus); try also *caldo gallego* (a hearty vegetable soup) and *empanada* (flaky pastry package stuffed with meat or seafood, served hot or cold).

Asturias: Look out for *fabada asturiana* (big white bean and sausage casserole), *merluza a la sidra* (hake in cider sauce), and *queso de Cabrales* (pungent, piquant, creamy blue cheese).

Basque country: Seafood is king here, in the form of *bacalao al pil pil* (fried cod in hot garlic sauce), *chipirones* (tiny squid), and *marmitako* (spicy tuna, tomato, and potato stew).

The Pyrenees: Hearty, warming meat dishes are served in *chilindrón* sauce (tomatoes, peppers, garlic, ham, and wine); look out for game dishes, and mountain trout.

Catalonia: This region is noted for *esqueixada* salad (grilled or baked vegetables in olive oil), grilled fish with *romesco* sauce (nuts, chili, tomatoes, garlic, and breadcrumbs), and seafood stews, like *zarzuela* and *suquet de Peix*.

Castile: Try *sopa castellana* for starters (a baked garlic soup with chunks of ham and an egg poaching in it), then *cochinillo asado* (suckling pig) or *cordero asado* (roast lamb).

The east coast: Valencia is the original home of *paella*, also try *arroz con costra* (rice with pork meatballs).

La Mancha: Quixote country is famed for such game dishes as *tojunto* (rabbit stew), but also for *pisto manchego* (an extravagant ratatouille-like vegetable stew with aubergines, tomatoes, and courgettes) and *queso manchego*, Spain's favorite cheese.

Extremadura: The region is noted for country-style pork and lamb and countless varieties of sausage.

Andalucía: Specialties include *gazpacho* and *ajo blanco* (or *gazpacho blanco*, made from garlic and almonds garnished with grapes), *fritura mixta* or *pescaito frito* (pieces of fish fried in a light batter), and *huevos a la flamenca* (egg, tomato, and vegetable baked with chorizo, prawns, and ham).

The islands: Canarian specialities include *papas arrugadas* (new potatoes baked and rolled in rock salt) served with *mojo picón* (piquant red sauce) and *mojo verde* (green herb sauce served with fish). On Mallorca, sample *tumbet* (ratatouille and potato casserole with meat or fish).

Sweet-Tooth Specials

The ubiquitous Spanish dessert is the egg-based *flan* (*crème caramel*). The Catalans do a deluxe version, *crema catalana*, which is flavored with lemon and cinnamon, and many towns have their own recipes for *yemas*, a monumentally sweet egg-yolk and sugar confection.

Otherwise, you can head for the *pastelerías* (cake shops) for a vast repertoire of cakes, tarts, and pastries. *Mazapan* (marzipan) and *turrón* (nougat) also come in various guises with regional variations.

WHAT TO DRINK

Wines and Alcoholic Drinks

Spain has more square kilometres of vineyards than any other European country. Vintage pundits confidently compare the best Spanish wines with the most respected French classics, causing controversy in some global wine circles. On the other hand, much of the crop is ordinary, intended for home consumption and never meant to grace the glasses of experts.

Spanish bodegas allow you to sample a range of the country's best wines.

The better Spanish wines are regulated by the *Denominación de Origen* quality control. If a bottle is marked DOC, you can be sure the wine was made in a particular region and its producers followed the strictest rules.

Regarding table wine, the oldest and most vigorously protected *denominación* is Rioja, and some truly distinguished reds (*tinto*) are grown along the Ebro valley in northern Spain. East of La Rioja, Aragon contributes some powerful Cariñena reds. The best-known wines from central Spain, the splendidly smooth reds of Valdepeñas, come from La Mancha.

The Penedés region of Catalonia is acclaimed not only for its excellent still wines, largely whites (*blanco*), but also for its *cava*, a sparkling wine made by the *methode champenoise*, an ennervating and refreshing chilled drink.

In the southwest, Jerez de la Frontera is the home of sherry. As an aperitif, try a chilled, dry *fino* or medium-dry *amontillado*. A dark, sweet *oloroso* goes down well after dinner. Spain also produces several sweet dessert wines, such as *moscatel*, which tastes of sultanas and honey.

Spanish brandy is often sweeter and heavier than French Cognac. It is a vital ingredient in *sangría* — probably the most popular tourist drink in Spain — whose other ingredients are red wine, orange and lemon juice, mineral water, sugar, sliced fruit, and ice.

Beer (*cerveza*) is generally of the pils, or lager, variety, and not very strong. There are plenty of Spanish brands, and foreign beers are widely available. A small draught beer is *una caña pequeña*, a medium size one is a *tubo* and a large one — a *grande* — is about the same size as a pint. Bottled beer is sold in a one-third liter bottle — *una botella* — or a one-quarter liter bottle — *una botellin*. Bottles are more expensive than draught, and not usually as cold.

Tea, Coffee, and Soft Drinks

The Spanish usually drink coffee (*café*) as opposed to tea (*té*). This can be either *solo*, small and black; *con leche*, a large cup made with milk; or *cortado*, a tiny cup with a little milk. Spanish coffee is nearly always strong. If you prefer it weaker, ask for *nescafé*.

Mineral water (*agua mineral*) is either sparkling (*con gas*) or still (*sin gas*). Ice cream parlors (*heladería*) sell *granizado*, slushy iced fruit juices, and fresh orange juice (*zumo de naranjas naturales*), though the latter can be surprisingly expensive considering oranges are one of Spain's main crops.

To Help You Order...

Could we have a table?	**¿Nos puede dar una mesa?**
Do you have a set menu?	**¿Tiene un menú del día?**
Id like a/an/some…	**Quisiera…**

beer	**una cerveza**	milk	**leche**
bread	**pan**	mineral water	**agua mineral**
coffee	**un café**	potatoes	**patatas**
dessert	**un postre**	rice	**arroz**
fish	**pescado**	salad	**una ensalada**
fruit	**fruta**	sandwich	**un bocadillo**
glass	**un vaso**	sugar	**azúcar**
ice cream	**un helado**	tea	**un té**
meat	**carne**	water (iced)	**agua (fresca)**
menu	**la carta**	wine	**vino**

...and Read the Menu

aceitunas	olives	**langosta**	spiny lobster
albóndigas	meatballs	**langostino**	large prawn

almejas	baby clams	**lomo**	loin
atún	tuna	**mariscos**	shellfish
anchoas	anchovies	**mejillones**	mussels
bacalao	codfish	**melocotón**	peach
besugo	sea bream	**merluza**	hake
boquerones	fresh anchovies	**navajas**	razor clams
calamares	squid	**ostras**	oysters
callos	tripe	**pastel**	cake
caracoles	snails	**pollo**	chicken
cerdo	pork	**pulpitos**	baby octopus
chuleta	chops	**salsa**	sauce
cocido	stew	**sepia**	squid
cordero	lamb	**ternera**	veal
entremeses	hors-d'oeuvre	**tortilla**	omelet
gambas	prawns	**trucha**	trout
habas	beans	**uvas**	grapes

Tapas

A *tapa* is a small portion of food, usually served with a slice or two of French bread, which encourages you to keep drinking instead of heading off to a restaurant for a meal. Once upon a time, *tapas* were given away, but that is rare these days. Even so, bars that specialize in *tapas* are more popular than ever.

Good *tapas* bars have a whole counter displaying hot and cold dishes, making it easy to make a choice — just point to one you like the look of. Typical offerings are olives, meatballs, local cheese, prawns in garlic, marinated anchovies, *chorizo* (spicy sausage), and wedges of Spanish *tortilla* (omelette). *Una tapa* is the smallest amount you can order; *una ración* is half a small plateful; and *una porción* is almost a meal in itself.

HANDY TRAVEL TIPS
An A–Z Summary of Practical Information

A

ACCOMMODATION *(hotel; alojamiento)* (See also CAMPING, YOUTH HOSTELS, and the list of recommended HOTELS AND RESTAURANTS)

Those travelling independently will find a wide range of options. For a comprehensive listing of accommodation and rates throughout Spain, consult the *Guía Oficial de Hoteles,* available from The Spanish National Tourist Office (see TOURIST INFORMATION OFFICES on page 169) and some local bookshops.

By law, prices must be displayed in the reception and in the room. Meals (including breakfast) are not usually included in the basic price, and VAT (IVA in Spanish) will be added to your bill.

Establishments are graded by each of the 17 autonomous governments, according to the following system, with one of the following ratings plus the number of stars:

Hotel (H): rated one to five stars according to services offered. The most expensive option, topped only by Hotel 5-star Gran Lujo (GL), signifying absolutely top-of-the-range accommodation.

Hotel Residencia (HR): same as a hotel, but there is no restaurant.

Motel (M): rated same as hotels, but in reality these are few and far between.

Hotel Apartamentos (HA): apartments within hotels, and rated the same as hotels.

Residencia Apartamentos (RA): residential apartments without a restaurant, rated the same as hotels.

Hostal (Hs): a more modest hotel, often a family concern, graded one to three stars. Rates overlap with the lower range of hotels, e.g, a three-star *hostal* costs about the same as a one or two-star hotel.

Spain

Hostal Residencia (HsR): as for a *hostal*, but without a restaurant.

Pensión (P): a boarding house, graded one to three stars, with only basic amenities.

Fonda (F): a small inn, fairly inexpensive, clean and unpretentious.

Casa de Huéspedes (CH): a guesthouse. Bottom of the scale, but usually clean and comfortable as well as cheap.

Ciudad de Vacaciones (CV): a hotel complex complete with sports facilities.

Casa Rural: a country house offering bed-and-breakfast or self-catering accommodation.

Parador: a state-run hotel, often housed in a castle or other historic building, of special interest to motorists, since they are generally located outside of towns in rural areas. Advance booking is not essential, but is highly recommended. For information and bookings in the USA and Canada contact Marketing Ahead, 433 Fifth Avenue, New York, NY, Tel. 1 800 223-1356 or (212) 686-9213, fax. (212) 686—0271 and e-mail <mahrep@aol.com>. In Spain contact the Paradores de Turismo, Central de Reservas, Requena, 3, 28013 Madrid, Tel. (91) 516 66 66, fax. (91) 516 66 57 or <www.parador.es>; in the UK, Tel. (020) 7402-8181, fax (020) 7724-9503.

I'd like a single/double room with bath/shower.	**Quisiera una habitación sencilla/doble con baño/ducha.**
What's the rate per night?	**¿Cuál es el precio por noche?**

AIRPORTS (*aeropuertos*) (See also GETTING THERE)
Madrid's Barajas airport (14 km/9 miles northeast of the capital) is the main gateway to Spain from North America, along with Barcelona and Málaga. Other important international airports are Alicante, Almería, Jerez de la Frontera, Santiago de Compostela, Sevilla and Valencia.

Madrid is Spain's main air transport hub, and airlines like IBERIA and Spanair offer frequent connections to regional airports throughout the country and to the Canary Islands and the Balearics.

B

BUDGETING FOR YOUR TRIP

To give you an idea of what to expect, here's a list of some average prices in Euros. They can only be approximate, however, as prices vary from place to place, and inflation in Spain, as elsewhere, creeps up relentlessly. Prices quoted may be subject to IVA, at variable rates.

Accommodation. Rates for a double room can range from as low as €24–€30 at a *pensión* or *hostal* to as much as €360–€420, or even more, at a top-of-the-range 5-star hotel. As a rule of thumb a good 4-star hotel will cost in the range of €90–€120.

Car rental. Prices vary dramatically according to a variety of factors: whether you rent before your trip starts; whether you rent from a company in your own country or locally; how long you want the car for; whether you want an automatic or manual transmission; what insurance cover you want, or are obliged, to purchase. If you want a small, manual-transmission car primarily for local use, then it may be cheaper to rent from a small local company, especially on the Costas and the islands. However, if you live in North America and are planning on touring around, will need a more reliable service or require a car with automatic transmission, then **auto-europe**, Tel. 1 800 223 555, offers good rates.

Entertainment. Cinema from €3.60, flamenco nightclub (entry and first drink) from €18, discotheque from €6. Amusement park (per day) €24 adult or €18 child. Bullfight €18–€90.

Spain

Meals and drinks. These vary considerably, according to where you choose to eat. In a bar a Continental breakfast, say fresh orange juice and toast, will cost around €3. The cheapest three-course meal with one drink, *menú del día*, in a small bar/restaurant will be around €5.40–€6.00. Dinner in a medium-level restaurant will be about €18 per head, including wine. At the top restaurants expect to pay €36–€42 per person, or more, plus wine. In a bar a small bottle or glass of beer will range from €0.60 to €0.90, coffee from €0.60 to €0.90, Spanish brandy €1.50 to €1.80, soft drinks from €0.90 and a glass of local wine about €0.45.

Shopping bag. Prices can vary substantially, according to where you shop. By far the cheapest places are the very large hypermarkets like Pryca where, for example, a can of San Miguel beer might cost around €0.40. In a small corner store or *supermercado* (supermarket) that same beer might cost between €0.60 and €0.75, and similar price differentials exist for most other goods.

Sightseeing. Admission prices for most museums are quite reasonable, usually between €1.50–€3.00, although this can be more in some places or even free in others. There are often student discounts and, sometimes, free entry to EC citizens.

Sports. Golf (per day) green fees range from around €45 up to as much as €180 at the very top courses. Tennis-court fees start at around €6 per hour. Horseback-riding starts at about €12 per hour.

Taxis. Taxis are generally inexpensive, with a typical city center ride costing around €2.40–€3.00 on the meter, with the rate for long distance journeys being agreed beforehand.

C

CAMPING *(camping)*

Spanish campgrounds are divided into categories, and rates and facilities vary accordingly. All sites, however, have drinking water, toilets and showers, electricity and basic first-aid facilities and all are under surveillance night and day. Rates depend to a large extent on the facilities available. For a complete list of campsites, consult the *Guía de Campings*, available from the Spanish National Tourist Office (see Tourist Information Offices on page 169) and some local bookshops.

Camping outside of official sites is permitted, provided you obtain permission from the landowner. However, you are not allowed to pitch your tent on tourist beaches, in urban areas, or within 1 km (½ mile) of an official site.

CAR HIRE *(coches de alquiler)* (See also Driving)

Renting a car before you go can avoid any uncertainties, and **auto europe**, Tel. 1 800 223.555, web site <www.autoeurope.com> is the largest organization operating in North America and more often than not offers the best rates available — especially so if you require a car with an automatic transmission. Otherwise, there are numerous car-hire firms in Spain, including all the major companies at the airports and some railway stations, but rates and conditions vary enormously. CDW insurance cover should be considered a necessity, and if your credit card doesn't include it, then purchase it from the car hire company. Theft from cars is rampant, and extra cover against theft of radio and other car parts, and damage caused by thieves, is very reasonable and seriously worth considering.

Normally you must be over 21 to hire a car, and you will need a valid driver's license that you have held for at least 12 months, your passport, and a major credit card — cash deposits are prohibitively large. Visitors from countries other than the US, Canada and those in the EU may be expected to present an International Driver's License.

Spain

I'd like to hire a car (tomorrow).	**Quisiera alquilar un coche (para mañana).**
for one day/a week	**por un día/una semana**
Please include full insurance.	**Haga el favor de incluir el seguro a todo riesgo.**

CLIMATE

As a general rule, late spring to early summer and late summer to early autumn are the best times for visiting most parts of Spain. This avoids the most oppressive heat, not to mention the crowds and high-season hotel rates. In winter, temperatures plummet in the high central plains.

Summer temperatures in the north are ideal for swimming and sunbathing, but expect rain any time in the northwest. At the height of summer (July–August) even the locals try to escape the dry, merciless heat of Madrid and the central plains; the southern and east coast areas can be uncomfortably humid.

For winter sun, head for the Canary Islands where temperatures rarely fall below a monthly average of 17°C (62°F). On the mainland, the south coast and parts of the central and southeastern coast are pleasantly mild year-round, but swimming is not really an option. Of course, winter is the best time for skiing in the Pyrenees, Picos de Europa, and Andalucía's Sierra Nevada.

CLOTHING

If you're heading for the south coast in the height of summer, pack loose cotton clothes and remember to take sun hats and sun-care lotion. In April, May, and October, you may need a light pullover for the evenings. From November to March, you should enjoy shirt-sleeve sunshine during the day, but this can be interrupted by chill winds from the mountains.

Winter visitors to Madrid and the central plains region will need to pack warm clothing. If you're heading for the northwest at any time, take waterproof gear.

Dress codes are very casual in most resorts, but tourists sporting resort wear in a big, sophisticated city like Madrid or Barcelona may attract stares. The Spanish enjoy dressing up for an occasion, and it is as well to look smart if you are visiting a good restaurant or reputable nightclub. Short skirts, shorts and beachwear are considered inappropriate attire for visits to churches, so carry a wrap to cover bare arms and legs.

COMPLAINTS

By law, all hotels and restaurants must have official complaint forms (*hoja de reclamaciones*) and produce them on demand. The original of this triplicate document should be sent to the Ministry of Tourism; one copy remains with the establishment involved and one copy is given to you. The very action of asking for the *hoja* may resolve the problem in itself, as the establishment knows that tourism authorities take a serious view of such complaints.

CRIME

Spain's crime rate has increased in recent years, especially in the major cities and some of the larger resorts. Here are a few precautions. Always carry a minimum of cash and keep your passport, traveler's checks, credit cards and cash in a money belt or, better still, in your hotel safe. Never leave bags unattended or out of reach.

The most common crime against the tourist in Spain is theft from rental cars. If you park overnight in the street in one of the big towns or resorts, there is every chance your car will be broken into. Always look for secure parking areas. Lock your car and stow any possessions out of sight in the boot (trunk), and never leave anything in your car overnight.

All thefts must be reported to the police within 24 hours. You will need a copy of the police report in order to make a claim on your holiday insurance.

As a precaution, photocopy the relevant pages of your passport(s) and airline ticket(s) and keep them in a separate place from the originals. This will save much time in the event of them being stolen. If this happens your consulate should also be informed (see EMBASSIES AND CONSULATES on page 158).

CUSTOMS *(aduana)* and ENTRY FORMALITIES
Most visitors, including citizens of all EU countries, the USA, Canada, Australia, and New Zealand, require only a valid passport to enter Spain. Visitors from South Africa must have a visa, which can be obtained from the Spanish Consulate General, 37 Short Market Street, Cape Town, 8001; Tel. (27) 21 422-2415; fax. (27) 21 422-2328; open Monday to Friday 8am to 1:30pm. The Internet site <www.raipttp.co.za/cargo/visa/cana-cpt.html> also gives full details of visa requirements.

Currency restrictions. Tourists may bring an unlimited amount of currency into the country.

DRIVING
Drive on the right, pass (overtake) on the left. Give way to traffic coming from the right.

Road conditions. Main roads and motorways are generally very good and improving all the time, secondary roads less so.

Rules and regulations. Speed limits are 50 km/h (30 mph) in built-up areas, 90–100 km/h (55–60 mph) on highways, and 120 km/h (75 mph) on motorways. Note that Spanish drivers tend to sound their horn or flash their headlights when overtaking. The use of seat belts (front and back seats) is obligatory. A red warning-triangle must be carried. Motorcycle riders and their passengers must wear crash helmets.

Spanish roads are patrolled by the motorcycle police of the Civil Guard (Guardia Civil). They can impose on-the-spot fines for minor offences including speeding, travelling too close to the car in front, and driving with deficient lights.

Fuel and oil. Service stations are plentiful, but it's a good idea to keep an eye on the gauge in the more remote areas and on Sundays.

Parking (*aparcamiento*). Parking regulations are strictly enforced — offending vehicles will be towed away, and a hefty fine charged for their return. A yellow-painted kerb means parking is prohibited at all times. Blue means parking is restricted to certain times and that you have to pay for and display a sticker inside your window, usually obtained from a nearby machine

Fluid measures

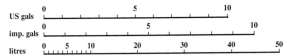

Distance

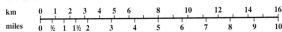

Road signs. Most of the road signs used in Spain are international pictograms. Here are some written signs you will come across:

Autopista (de peaje)	(Toll) motorway (expressway)
Ceda el paso	Give way (Yield)
Circunvalación	Bypass/ring-road
Curva peligrosa	Dangerous bend
Despacio	Slow
Desviación	Diversion (Detour)
Obras	Road works
Peligro	Danger
Prohibido aparcar	No parking
Salida de camiones	Lorry (Truck) exit
Sin plomo	Unleaded petrol

¿Se puede aparcar aquí?	Can I park here?
Llénelo, por favor, con super.	Full tank, please, top grade.
Por favor, controle el aceite/ los neumáticos/la batería.	Check the oil/tyres/battery.
Ha habido un accidente.	There's been an accident.

E

ELECTRICITY

220V/50Hz AC (*corriente eléctrica*) is now standard, but older installations of 125 volts can still be found. An adapter for Continental-style two-pin sockets will be needed; American 110V appliances will also require a transformer.

EMBASSIES and CONSULATES *(embajadas y consulados)*

All embassies (a selection of which are listed below) are in Madrid, and many countries have consular facilities in large cities such as Barcelona and Sevilla, as well as in resort areas popular with foreign tourists such as the Costa del Sol and Palma, the capital of Mallorca. If you run into trouble with the authorities or the police, the embassy can advise you where to find the nearest consulate.

Australia: Plaza Desc. Diego de Ordás 3, 2nd Floor;
Tel. (91) 441 93 00.

Canada: Núñez de Balboa 35; Tel. (91) 431 43 00.

Republic of Ireland: Paseo de la Castellano, 46; Tel. (91) 576 35 09.

South Africa: Claudio Coello 91; Tel. (91) 435 66 88.

UK: Fernando el Santo 16; Tel. (91) 319 02 08.

US: Serrano 75; Tel. (91) 587 22 00.

EMERGENCIES *(emergencias)*

Unless you are fluent in Spanish you should seek help through your hotel receptionist or the local tourist office. If you can speak Spanish, the following telephone numbers may be useful.

Ambulance	Police	Sea Rescue
061	091	900 202202

ETIQUETTE

The Spanish are still, by and large, an easy-going, friendly people, but they still, mostly, share a belief in the virtues of mañana: never do today what you can put off until tomorrow. There is no point in trying to rush them either. Far from making things better, it might lengthen the delay.

Politeness and simple courtesies do still matter here. Always begin a conversation with *buenos días* (good morning), *buenas tardes* (good afternoon) or *buenas noches* (good evening), and sign off with *adiós* (goodbye) when leaving. And a handshake never goes amiss. One of the most enjoyable features of Spanish everyday life is the evening *paseo* when young and old alike come out to take a stroll, see and be seen, and build up an appetite for supper.

When eating in a restaurant, you must always ask for the bill. It is very rarely offered, as no waiter wishes to be seen to be actually encouraging you to leave. Since a service charge is normally included in both hotel and restaurant bills, tipping is not obligatory — but if the service was good, you might leave around 10 percent of the bill.

When sightseeing, dress respectfully for visits to churches, and don't forget the sacred Spanish siesta when planning your itinerary. Many museums and attractions, as well as shops and businesses, are firmly closed from around 1 or 2pm until 4 or 5pm.

Children are always welcome just about wherever you go in Spain — including bars and restaurants — and everyone likes to make a fuss of them.

G

GETTING THERE

By air from North America. Iberia, Tel. 1 800 772-4642; <www.iberia.com> has flights from New York City and Miami to Madrid, and connections from there to Málaga, Sevilla and other smaller airports, air europa, Tel. (718) 244-7055; fax. (718) 656 04 08; <www.air-europa.com> has flights from New York City to Madrid, and connections from there to Málaga, Sevilla and other smaller airports. It also has a weekly scheduled flight between New York City and Málaga, in each direction. Spanair, Tel. 1 888 545 57 57 or <www.spainair.com>, flies out of Washington DC and has flights to Madrid with onward connections to most destinations. Spanair also offers the economical Spain Pass, good for travel on the mainland and the Canary Islands.

By air from Europe. Scheduled flights link major European cities directly to the most important cities, and charter flights arrive in their hundreds from numerous destinations in northern Europe.

By car. From the UK, the main route from the French ferry ports runs south through western France to Bordeaux and into Spain at Irún, west of the Pyrenees. Alternatively, take the eastern route through France to Perpignan in the southeast, then you can follow the A7 motorway to Barcelona and other points south.

Driving time can be cut by using the long-distance car-ferry service from Plymouth to Santander and Portsmouth to Bilbao in northern Spain.

By rail. From the UK, take the high speed Eurostar (<www.eurostar.com>) from London's Waterloo International, through the Channel Tunnel to Lille. French National Railways, SNCF (<www.sncf.com>) operate high-speed TGV trains from either Gare Montparnasse or Gare d'Orleans in Paris to the French/Spanish border at Hendaye/Irún or Cerbere/Port Bou, on the western and eastern sides of the Pyrenees respectively. From either of those places change to a Spanish train (<www.renfe.es>) and head for your destination of choice.

By sea. From the UK, two companies offer car ferry services to mainland Spain, with schedules varying by the season. Brittany Ferries, Tel. 0870 9012400, has sailings with an average crossing time of 24hrs between Plymouth and Santander and P&O European Ferries, Tel. 0870 2424999, has sailings with an average crossing time of 35hrs between Portsmouth and Bilbao.

GUIDES and TOURS

An English-speaking guide can be contacted through most local tourist offices. Tourist offices can also provide details of city walking tours and bus-tour operators in their area. They can assist with itineraries and may arrange bookings for you, possibly for a nominal fee. Guided tours and excursions can also be booked through your hotel reception in most resort areas and large cities, and through numerous travel agencies (*agencia de viaje*). Check at the time of booking that your guide will be able to speak your language.

 H

HEALTH & MEDICAL

Anything other than basic emergency treatment can be very expensive, and you should not leave home without adequate insurance, preferably including cover for an emergency flight home in the event of serious injury or illness.

EU citizens are entitled to free emergency hospital treatment — you should obtain form E111 from a post office before you leave in order to qualify. You may have to pay part of the price of treatment or medicines; keep receipts so that you can claim a refund when you return home.

One of the main health hazards is also Spain's biggest attraction — the sun. Take along a sun hat, sunglasses, and plenty of high-factor sunscreen, and limit your sunbathing sessions to an hour or less until you begin to tan.

Spain

For minor ailments, visit the local first-aid post (*ambulatorio*). Away from your hotel, don't hesitate to ask the police or a tourist information office for help. At your hotel, ask the staff for assistance. *Farmacias* (chemist/drugstore) are usually open during normal shopping hours. After hours, at least one per town remains open all night; called a *farmacia de guardia*, its location is posted in the window of all other chemists and in the local newspapers.

Where's the nearest (all-night) chemist?	**¿Dónde está la farmacia (de guardia) más cercana?**
I need a doctor/dentist.	**Necesito un médico/dentista.**
sunburn/sunstroke	**quemadura del sol/una insolación**
an upset stomach	**molestias de estómago**

HOLIDAYS *(días festivos)*

Banks, post offices, government offices, and many other businesses will be closed on the following dates. Note that there are also a number of local and regional holidays and saint's days; check with the local tourist office.

1 January	*Año Nuevo*	New Year's Day
6 January	*Epifanía*	Epiphany
19 March	*San José*	St Joseph's Day
March/April	*Jueves Santo*	Maundy Thursday
	Viernes Santo	Good Friday
11 May	*Día del Trabajo*	Labor Day
May/June	*Corpus Christi*	Corpus Christi
25 July	*Santiago Apóstol*	St James's Day
15 August	*Asunción*	Feast of the Assumption
12 October	*Día de la Hispanidad*	Columbus Day
1 November	*Todos los Santos*	All Saints' Day
6 December	*Día de la Constitución*	Constitution Day
8 December	*Immaculada Concepción*	Immaculate Conception
25 December	*Día de Navidad*	Christmas Day

LANGUAGE

The national language of Spain, Castilian Spanish, is spoken throughout the country. However, it is estimated that two out of every five Spaniards speak another language primarily, and this trend has been especially marked since the decentralization of some political powers to the regions. The inhabitants of the Basque Country, Galicia, Catalonia, and the Balearics speak Euskara, Gallego, Catalan and variants of Catalan, respectively. More confusing still are local dialects of Castilian such as Andaluz spoken throughout Andalucía, which is a little more difficult to understand than Spanish.

English is widely spoken in the resort towns, though it is polite to learn at least a few basic phrases. The Berlitz *Spanish Phrasebook and Dictionary* covers most situations you are likely to encounter, and the Berlitz Spanish-English/English-Spanish pocket dictionary contains some 12,000 entries, plus a menu-reader supplement.

LOST PROPERTY (*objetos perdidos*) (See also CRIME on page 155)
For items left behind on public transport, ask your hotel receptionist to telephone the bus or train station or taxi company. Then check with the hotel reception for the address of any local lost property offices. If you still cannot find the missing item, then report the loss to the Municipal Police or the Guardia Civil within 24-hours (see POLICE). They will issue you a form that you will need if you wish to make an insurance claim once you are home.

M

MEDIA

Radio and television (*radio; televisión*). Depending upon where you are it is possible, most especially on the Costas and in the Canary Islands and parts of the Balearics, to find radio stations that broadcast in English on the FM band. Network television programs are all in Spanish, but better hotels and many English bars also have satellite TV with CNN, MTV, Superchannel, Sky TV, etc.

Newspapers and magazines (*periódico, revista*). In the major tourist areas you can buy most European newspapers on the day of publication, with some English ones even having Spanish editions, but at about three times the price. The *International Herald Tribune* is also widely available as are British and American magazines. In the Costas and the islands there are any number of weekly/monthly English language newspapers and magazines, some of which are free.

MONEY MATTERS

Currency. The monetary unit of Spain is the euro; with one hundred cents making 1 euro. Coins: cents 1, 2, 5, 10, 20, and 50, and euros 1 and 2. Banknotes: euros 5, 10, 20, 50, 100, 200 and 500. The euro is roughly equivalent to US$1.

Outside normal banking hours, many travel agencies and other businesses displaying a *cambio* sign will change foreign currency into Euros. All larger hotels will also change guests' money. The exchange rate is slightly less than at the bank. Traveler's checks always get a better rate than cash. You must take your passport with you when changing money or traveler's checks. ATM machines can be found everywhere.

Credit cards and traveler's checks. These are accepted in most hotels, restaurants, and big shops.

VAT (*IVA*). Remember that IVA (*impuesto sobre el valor agregado*), the Spanish equivalent of value added tax, will be added to your hotel and restaurant bills; it currently stands at 7 percent. A higher rate of 16 percent applies to car-hire charges and a rate of 4 percent applies to certain basic necessities. In the Canary Islands this is known as IGIC and levied at a rate of 4.5 percent on hotel rooms.

O

OPENING HOURS

Shops and offices and other businesses generally observe the afternoon siesta, opening 9:30am/10am to 1:30pm/2pm, and 4:30pm/5pm to 7:30pm/8pm, but in tourist areas many places now stay open all day. Banks are generally open from 9am to 2pm, but beware of the numerous public holidays.

P

POLICE *(policía)*

There are three separate police forces in Spain. The Policía Municipal are attached to the local town hall and usually wear a blue uniform; they are the ones to whom you report theft and other crimes. The Policía Nacional is a national anti-crime unit who wear a dark blue uniform; and the Guardia Civil, with green uniforms, is a national force whose most conspicuous role is to act as a highway patrol. Spanish police, often working in pairs, are generally very courteous and helpful towards foreign visitors.

The emergency number is 911.

POST OFFICES *(correos)*

Post offices (<www.correos.es>) handle mail and telegrams only. You cannot normally make telephone calls from them. Hours vary slightly from town to town, but routine postal business is generally transacted from 8:30am to 2:30pm, Monday to Friday, and 9:30am to 1pm on Saturday. Postage stamps *(sellos)* are also on sale at tobacconists *(estancos)* and hotel desks, and at tourist shops selling postcards. Mail for destinations outside Spain should be posted in the box marked *extranjero* (overseas), and delivery is slow.

Spain

PUBLIC TRANSPORTATION

Buses (*autobús*). These are cheap, reasonably comfortable, and reliable in most areas, but beware of drastically reduced timetables on Sundays. There are extensive bus services within and between major cities, but in the countryside services generally only run into and out of provincial centers — so links to smaller towns and resorts may not be possible, even if they are quite close by. They often go to destinations that are not served by trains, and are more often than not cheaper, faster and more frequent than trains.

Ferries (*barcos*). These are a necessary form of transport from the mainland to Ceuta and Tangiers — on the North African coast, and between the Canary and Balearic islands themselves and, to a lesser extent, to and from the Canary Islands and the Balearics. Trasmediterránea, (<www.trasmediterranea.com>) is the largest company operating ferry services in Spain.

Taxis (*taxi*). In the major cities, taxis have meters, but in smaller towns and villages they usually don't, so it's a good idea to check the fare before you get in. If you take a long trip, you will be charged a two-way fare whether you make the return journey or not. By law a taxi may carry only four persons. A green light and/or a *Libre* (free) sign indicates a taxi that is available.

Trains (*tren*). Madrid is the hub of the complicated RENFE (Spanish National Railways) network, which reaches out like a spider's web to most corners of the country. There are a bewildering number of different types of train service, from all-stops local services (*cercanías*) to the high-speed AVE that makes the trip from Madrid to Sevilla in just two hours and a half.

Timetables and information are available from railway stations and tourist offices, and from the RENFE Internet web site, <www.renfe.es>.

The Spain Flexipass gives you 3 days of unlimited rail travel (in 1st or 2nd class) starting at US$155 (2nd class). Additional rail days are US$30 (2nd class) and US$35 (1st class) each. The Spain Rail 'n' Drive Pass gives you 3 days of unlimited rail travel plus 2 days of car rental. Prices depend on class of rail travel and car category (four categories are available) and start at US$255 per person for two traveling together.

For information on the Spain Flexipass, Spain Rail 'n' Drive Pass, and point-to-point rail tickets on Spanish trains, including the high-speed Euromed (Barcelona, Valencia, Alicante) or AVE (Madrid, Córdoba, Sevilla, Cádiz, Málaga) trains, contact Rail Europe at Tel. 1 888 382-7245 or <www.raileurope.com>, *before* you arrive in Europe. The web site also contains useful rail trip planning information, especially the section on "Fares and Schedules".

Where is the (nearest) bus stop?	**¿Dónde está la parada de autobuses (más cercana)?**
When's the next bus/boat for…?	**¿A qué hora sale el próximo autobús/barco para…?**
I want a ticket to…	**Quiero un billete para…**
single (one-way)	**ida**
return (round-trip)	**ida y vuelta**
Will you tell me when	**¿Podría indicarme cuándo**
to get off?	**tengo que bajar?**

R

RELIGION

The national religion is Roman Catholicism. In the main tourist centers, services are held in various languages. There are Protestant churches and Jewish synagogues in most major cities, but services will still be held in Spanish unless there is a large resident English-speaking contingent in town, as there is on the Costa del Sol, for example.

T

TELEPHONES *(teléfonos)*

The country code for Spain is 34.

There are phone booths in all major towns and cities from which you can make local and international calls. Instructions in English and area codes for different countries are displayed in the booths. International calls are expensive, so be sure to have a plentiful supply of coins. Some telephones accept credit cards, and many require a phone card *(tarjeta telefónica)*, available from *tabacos*. For international direct dialing, pick up the receiver, wait for the dial tone, then dial 07, wait for a second tone and dial the country code, area code (minus the initial zero) and number.

Remember, calling directly from your hotel room is almost always very expensive unless you use a calling card, or some other similar system, from your local long distance supplier — in which case find out from the supplier the free connection number applicable to the countries; they are different for each country and these numbers are not always easily available once you are there.

Another economic option is to use a private booth that advertises their prices for particular countries in the window or on boards outside. Their rates are usually highly competitive, and you pay at the completion of the call.

The number for the International Operator is 025.

The country code for the USA and Canada is 01; the UK 44; Australia 61; New Zealand 64; the Republic of Ireland 353; and South Africa 27.

Can you get me this number?   **¿Puede comunicarme con este número?**

TIME ZONES

Spanish time coincides with most of Western Europe — Greenwich Mean Time plus one hour. In summer, another hour is added for

Daylight Saving Time (Summer Time), keeping it an hour ahead of British Summer Time. Remember, the time in the Canary Islands is one hour earlier than on mainland Spain.

New York	London	Spain	Sydney	Auckland
6am	11am	noon	8pm	10pm

TOILETS/RESTROOMS

The most commonly used expressions for toilets are *servicios* or *aseos*, and the usual signs are *damas* for women and *caballeros* for men.

Public conveniences are rare, but all hotels, bars, and restaurants have toilets, usually of a reasonable standard, for the use of bona fide customers (often you will have to ask for a key).

TOURIST INFORMATION OFFICES *(oficina de turismo)*

Information about Spain may be obtained from one of the international branches of the Spanish National Tourist Offices listed below.

Australia: Level 2–203, Castlereagh Street, NSW, 2000 Sydney South, Tel. (2) 264-7966.

Canada: 2 Bloor Street West, 34th Floor, Toronto, Ontario M4W 3E2; Tel. (416) 961-3131, fax. (416) 961-1992, e-mail <spainto@globalserve.net>.

UK: 22-23 Manchester Square, London, W1M 5AP; Tel. (020) 7486 8077, fax. (020) 7486 8034, e-mail <buzon.oficial@londres.oet.mcx.es>.

US: Water Tower Place, Suite 915 East, 845 N. Michigan Avenue, Chicago, IL 60611; Tel. (312) 642-1992, fax. (312) 642-9817, e-mail <buzon.oficial@chicago.oet.mcx.es>.

8383 Wilshire Boulevard, Suite 960, Beverly Hills, Los Angeles, CA 90211; Tel. (213) 658 7188, fax. (323) 658-1061, e-mail <buzon.oficial@losangeles.oet.mcx.es>.

Spain

665 Fifth Avenue, New York, NY 10103; Tel. (212) 265-8822, fax. (212) 265-8864, e-mail <buzon.oficial@nuevayork.oetmcx.es>. 1221 Brickell Avenue, Miami, FL 33131; Tel. (305) 358-1992, fax. (305) 358-8223, e-mail <buzon.oficial@miami.oet.mcx.es>.

For further information check the Internet web site <www.tourspain.es>.

TRAVELERS WITH DISABILITIES

Facilities for travelers with disabilities are improving all the time, but as yet public transport is not wheelchair accessible. The Spanish National Tourist Office (see page 169) provides a fact sheet and a list of accessible accommodation. Remember, too, that many museums and other sights are not wheelchair accessible and a visit may require extensive walking.

Visually impaired travelers can contact ONCE, the Organización Nacional de Ciegos de España (Spanish National Organization for the Blind) Tel. (91) 431 1900.

W

WEB SITES

A good, general purpose, web site is <www.tourspain.es>. Regional websites are as follows:

Andalucía <www.andalucia.org>

Balearic Islands <www.balearics.com>

Barcelona <www.barcelonaturisme.com>

Basque Country <www.basquecountry-tourism>

Canary Islands <www.canary-isles.com>

Costa del Sol <www.costadelsol.sopde.es>

Madrid <www.comadrid.es/turismo>

Pamplona <www.pamplona.net>

Valencia <www.turisvalencia.es>

The sites for Castilla y León <www.jcyl.es> and Galicia <www.galinor.es> were in Spanish only in July 2001.

The <www.spainlist.com> site has numerous links to places and things throughout Spain.

WEIGHTS and MEASURES
For fluid and distance measures, see page 157.

Length

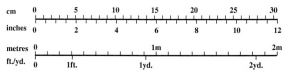

Weight

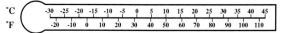

Temperature

Y

YOUTH HOSTELS *(albergues de juveniles)*
These are fairly few and far between, but you can get a list of Spanish youth hostels from the YHA or Spanish National Tourist Office. Many hostels operate in summer only, from temporary premises, such as schools, so make sure you have an up-to-date list. When there is nothing else available, look for a *fonda*. Fondas provide fairly basic rooms, but many enjoy convenient town-center locations. Some have rooms with three or four beds that are a bargain for those travelling in a group.

Recommended Hotels

The following hotels, a selection of accommodations in towns, cities, and resorts throughout Spain, are listed alphabetically, with their Spanish hotel ratings (see Accommodations page 149) given in brackets after each name. It is always advisable to reserve well in advance, particularly if you will be visiting in the high season — which can vary from destination to destination and often coincides with important fiestas.

Prices do not normally include breakfast. As a guide we have used the symbols below to indicate the price for a double room with bath or shower in the high season. Low season rates can be considerably lower.

€	€50–90
€€	€90–120
€€€	€120–180
€€€€	€180–300

ÁVILA

Hospedería La Sinagoga €€/€€€ *Reyes Católicos 22; Tel. (920) 35 23 21; fax 35 34 74*. In the 15th century this was one of the most important synagogues in Ávila. In the heart of the city, this has now been transformed into a unique and modern small hotel where each room is different from the others. 22 rooms.

BARCELONA

Gran Hotel Havana (4 stars) €€€/€€€€ *Gran Via Corts Catalanes 647; Tel. (93) 412 11 15; fax 412 26 11*. Founded in a charming house that dates from 1872, this was enlarged and renovated in 1991 into a deluxe hotel. It has an unusually shaped central atrium, around which are large, well-furnished modern rooms and suites, all sound-proofed and with 24-hour room service. 145 rooms.

Rivoli Ramblas (4 stars) €€€€ *La Rambla 128; Tel. (93) 481 76 76; fax 317 50 53*. Excellently situated on the famous La Rambla and close to Plaça Catalunya. Look for a combination of art-deco and avant-garde style in well-equipped soundproofed rooms. Fantastic views from the terrace, where there is also a fitness center and sauna. 90 rooms.

Hotel Condes de Barcelona (4 stars) €€€/€€€€ *Passeig de Gracia 73–75; Tel. (93) 467 47 86; fax 467 47 85*. Located in the business area, this occupies a couple of typically 19th-century Barcelona modernist structures and is a very popular hotel. Ask for a room with a jacuzzi. 109 rooms.

Hotel Mesón Castilla (2 stars) €/€€ *Valldoncella 5; Tel. (93) 318 21 82; fax 412 40 20*. A quiet dignified hotel located on the Plaça Castilla just a hundred yards or so from the Plaça Catulunya. Elegant public rooms and a private garage. 56 rooms.

BILBAO

Hotel López de Haro (5 stars) €€€/€€€€ *Obispo Orueta 2; Tel. (94) 423 55 00; fax 423 45 00*. The top hotel in Bilbao, this is located in a renovated 19th-century structure and offers a combination of a classical style with every latest facility. In the city center and close to the Guggenheim Museum, this also has a fine restaurant. 53 rooms.

CARMONA

Hotel Casa Palacio Casa de Carmona (5 stars) €€€ *Plaza de Lasso 1; Tel. (95) 414 33 00; fax 414 37 52; web site <www.casade-carmona.com>*. A 16th-century palace that has been carefully and lovingly renovated into a beautiful and very hospitable luxurious hotel. Every room is unique, and filled with handpicked antiques from Madrid, London and Paris. 33 rooms.

CÓRDOBA

Hotel NH Amistad Córdoba (4 stars) €€€ *Plaza Maimónides 3; Tel. (957) 42 03 35; fax 42 03 65.* Located in the Jewish quarter close to the Mezquita, two 18th-century mansions, next to the old Moorish wall, have been combined and restored to form a fully modernized hotel in harmony with this historic city. 84 rooms.

COSTA DEL SOL

Kempinski Resort Hotel (5 stars) €€€€ *Ctra. de Cádiz Km 159, Estepona; Tel. (95) 280 95 00; fax 280 95 50; web site <www.kempinski-spain.com>.* All rooms in this architecturally interesting hotel (opened September 1999) have a sea view. Guests also enjoy a marvelous subtropical garden, a 1-km beach, numerous pools, water-sports and horseback-riding facilities, a haute-cuisine restaurant and the Polly Mar Thalasso Wellness center. 149 rooms.

Hotel Sidi Lago Rojo (3 stars) €€ *Miami 5, La Carihuela; Tel. (95) 238 76 66; fax 238 0891; web site <www.hotelessidi.es>.* Found very close to the famous La Carihuela beach, this is a charming modern hotel with all modern facilities. 144 rooms.

GRANADA

Alhambra Palace (4 stars) €€€ *Peña Partida 2; Tel. (958) 22 14 68; fax 22 64 04.* An impressive and elaborate Moorish-style palace in the Alhambra Park complex, sitting on the edge of the hill, the Alhambra Palace has stunning views across the city and up to the Sierra Nevada. 144 rooms.

Hotel Palacio de Santa Inés (3 stars) €€€ *Cuesta de Santa Inés 9; Tel. (958) 22 23 62; fax 22 24 65.* The 16th-century palace known as the House of the Eternal Father has been beautifully converted into a hotel of considerable charm. It is located in the historic Albaicin area, on the opposite bank of the Darro to the towering Alhambra fortress. 6 rooms/6 suites.

LEÓN

Parador San Marcos (4 stars) €€€ *Plaza San Marcos 7; Tel. (987) 23 73 00; fax 23 34 58.* Housed in an amazingly decorative 16th-century former convent, with an impressive Spanish Renaissance period façade, this is one of Spain's finest and most luxurious *paradores*, as well as being a national monument. Ask for a room in the atmospheric old part, with its tapestry-lined walls. 253 rooms.

MADRID

Hesperia Madrid (5 stars) €€€€ *Paseo de la Castellana 57; Tel. (91) 210 88 00; fax 210 88 99.* This is a brand new contemporary-style hotel, the first of its kind in Madrid. Expect to find distinguished rooms and public areas, exemplary service, fine restaurants and a great location in cosmopolitan section of the city. 171 rooms.

Hotel Wellington (5 stars) €€€€ *Veláquez 8; Tel. (91) 575 44 00; fax 576 41 64.* This is a distinguished hotel in a distinguished location — close to the Prado and the Puerta de Alcála. All rooms have a classical décor combined with the latest in facilities. Fine restaurant and nice bar, too. 300 rooms.

Santo Domingo (4 stars) €€€ *Plaza de Santa Domingo 13; Tel. (91) 547 98 00; fax 547 59 95.* This is located in a quiet location not far from the Puerta del Sol. Each room has been personalized so that they are all different in style and décor. 120 rooms.

Arosa (4 stars) €€€ *Calle de la Salud 21; Tel. (91)532 16 00; fax 531 31 27.* Very centrally located, just off the Gran Vía and not far from the Puerta del Sol. Rooms range from the grand old style of the original building to sleek, modern quarters. Swimming pool. 126 rooms.

París (2 stars) € *Alcalá 2; Tel. (91) 521 64 96; fax 531 01 88.* Has a most central location, with a wonderful façade overlooking the Puerta del Sol. Traditional style and ambiance. 114 rooms.

MÉRIDA

Parador Vía de la Plata (4 stars) €€€ *Plaza de la Constitución 3; Tel. (924) 31 38 00; fax 31 92 08.* Located in what was once an 18th-century convent that, itself, was the site of a Roman Praetorian Guard Palace. An elegant mix of history and style. 82 rooms.

PAMPLONA

Avenida (3 stars) €€ *Avenida de Zaragoza 5; Tel. (948) 24 54 54; fax 23 23 23.* This has an unusual wedge-shaped façade and the balconies of this restored building overlook the fountain on Plaza Príncipe de Viana. As usual in Pamplona the rooms, although pleasant and comfortable, are not large. 24 rooms.

SALAMANCA

Rector (4 stars) €€€ *Paseo del Rector Esparabe 10; Tel. (923) 21 84 82; fax 21 40 08.* This magnificent structure was home to one of Salamanca's most aristocratic families. These days, it has been tastefully converted into a delightful small hotel.

SAN SEBASTIÁN

María Cristina (5 stars) €€€ *Paseo de la República Argentina 4; Tel. (943) 42 49 00; fax 42 39 14.* A grand *belle-époque* building dating from 1912 that used to be King Alfonso XIII's winter head-quarters. A renovation in 1987 added modern facilities and extra luxuries to this, the finest hotel in San Sebastián. 139 rooms.

SANTIAGO DE COMPOSTELA

Los Reyes Católicos (5 stars GL) €€€€ *Plaza del Obradoiro 1; Tel. (981) 58 22 00; fax 56 30 94.* Constructed by the Catholic Monarchs in the late 15th century, and later expanded in the 17th and 18th centuries, this is one of Spain's oldest and grandest hotels. Located on one of Spain's most magnificent squares, the parador combines history with modern facilities. 136 rooms.

SEGOVIA

Los Linajes (3 stars) €€ *Dr. Velasco 9; Tel. (921) 46 04 75; fax 46 04 79.* Just a two-minute walk from the Plaza Mayor, this is housed in a 17th-century building located on the edge of the old city and overlooking the countryside. Most rooms have a terrace. 105 rooms.

SEVILLA

Alfonso XIII (5 stars GL) €€€€ *San Fernando 2; Tel. (95) 422 28 50; fax 21 60 33.* Opened by King Alfonso XIII in 1929, this imposing hotel in the city center is set in its own lovely gardens and epitomizes Sevillian style and luxury. The spacious rooms are classically decorated and the lobby bar is a meeting point for Sevilla's high society. 149 rooms.

Hotel Los Seises (4 stars) €€€ *Segovias 6; Tel. (95) 422 94 95; fax 422 43 34.* This is a 16th-century palace where historic surroundings combine with modern facilities to create an intriguing ambiance. Located in the Barrio de Santa Cruz, it has a rooftop pool overlooking the nearby Cathedral and Giralda. 43 rooms.

Dona Maria (4 stars) €€€€ *Don Remonelo 19; Tel. (95) 422 49 40; fax 421 95 46.* A charming hotel with an interesting mix of antiques and modern facilities, and an excellent central location, with a rooftop pool and bar, almost within touching distance of the Giralda and Cathedral. 70 rooms.

Spain

Hotel Simón (2 stars) € *García de Vinuesa 19; Tel. (95) 422 66 60; fax 456 22 41.* A handsome hotel set in a renovated 18th-century townhouse, well situated just across from the cathedral. 31 rooms.

TOLEDO

Parador Conde de Orgaz (4 stars) €€/€€€ *Cerro del Emperador s/n; Tel. (925) 22 18 50; fax 22 51 66.* Comfortable rooms, a fine restaurant, traditional service and a pool — plus magnificent views over fabulously historic Toledo, which is floodlit at night. 77 rooms.

Pintor El Greco (3 stars) €€ *Alamillos del Tránsito 13; Tel. (925) 21 42 50; fax 21 58 19.* Delightful 17th-century house, with pleasant rooms, modern comforts and car parking, located in a charming section of the old town close to most monuments. 33 rooms.

VALENCIA

Hotel Sidi Saler (5 stars) €€€ *Playa El Saler: Tel. (96) 161 04 11; fax 161 08 38; web site <www.hotelessidi.es>.* This is as good as it gets: a wonderful hotel right on the Mediterranean with a fine restaurant and health spa, and a free bus into Valencia, 15 minutes away.

BALEARIC ISLANDS

IBIZA

Hacienda (5 stars) €€€€ *Miguel; Tel. (971) 33 45 00; fax 33 45 14.* Perched on high cliffs, dramatically overlooking the Mediterranean, this luxury hotel has the finest location on Ibiza. The décor is an intriguing mix of traditional Ibicenco style and art deco. 54 rooms.

Ca'spla €€€ *San Miguel de Balanzat; Tel. (971) 33 45 87; fax 33 46 04; web site <www.caspla-ibiza.com>.* Listed as a "Hotel Rural" this is at least as good as any 5-star hotel. Large and eclectically decorated rooms (some even with a private pool) are set in luxuriant grounds with wooden-beamed patios overlooking the pool.

Hostal Cala Moli (3 stars) €€ *Apartado 105, San Jose; Tel. (971) 80 60 02; fax 80 61 50.* Located in the quieter southeast of the island, this is a charming, small *hostal* with attractive views from the pool and patio out over the Mediterranean.

MALLORCA

Son Vida (5 stars GL) €€€€ *Son Vida; Tel. (971) 79 00 00; fax 79 00 17; web site <www.hsonvida.balears.net>.* 13th-century castle transformed in 1961 into a magnificent deluxe hotel. Palatial surroundings, unparalleled service, fine restaurants, fantastic views overlooking Palma de Mallorca and the Mediterranean, beautiful gardens, nearby golf courses and the city just 10 minutes away.

Formentor (5 stars GL) €€€/€€€€ *Formentor; Tel. (971) 89 91 00; fax 86 51 55; web site <www.fehm.es/pmi/formentor>.* In a fantastic location, possibly the best in the Balearics, surrounded by forests and with sculpted gardens leading onto a beautiful bay surrounded by mountains. A classical, formal hotel often frequented by famous personalities. Three restaurants and a health and beauty center.

La Reserva Rotana (4 stars) €€€ *Manacor-Mallorca: Tel. (971) 84 56 85; fax 55 52 58; web site <www.reservarotana.com>.* In the middle of a 20-hectare (500-acre) working farm close to Manacor, this is a 17th-century manor house and adjacent buildings tastefully converted into a luxury country estate. Huge rooms decorated with handpicked furniture and antiques, and a private 9-hole golf course.

MENORCA

Port Mahón (4 stars) €€ *Avenida Fort de l'Eau 13; Tel. (971) 36 26 00; fax 35 10 50.* A charming hotel with an attractive façade, and gardens with a pool, overlooking the wide expanse of the well-protected Mahón harbor. Nice size rooms, especially those with balconies overlooking the water. Swimming pool. 82 rooms.

CANARY ISLANDS

FUERTEVENTURA

Hotel Riu Palace Tres Islas (4 stars) €€/€€€ *Grandes Playas, Corralejo; Tel (928) 53 57 00; fax 53 58 58.* Perfectly located on the magnificent beach with a view of the dunes and Lanzarote. Very well appointed rooms, attractive pool and terrace, boutiques and nightly entertainment in the piano bar and Betancuria lounge. 365 rooms.

GRAN CANARIA

Steigenberger La Canaria (5 stars) €€€ *Arguineguin; Tel. (928) 15 04 00; fax 15 10 03; web site <www.steigenberger.com>.* One of the newest and most luxurious hotels on the south coast. Cut into a cliff with its own private gardens, access to beaches, gourmet restaurant and health center, this has excellent facilities and breathtaking sea views. 244 rooms.

Hotel Club de Mar (3 stars) €€ *Urbanización Puerto de Mogán s/n, Playa de Mogán; Tel. (928) 56 50 66; fax 56 54 38; web site <www.clubdemar.com>.* Enjoys an absolutely wonderful location at the end of the harbor in this delightful marina. Pleasant rooms with all the expected facilities, plus pool and bar and swimming in the harbor. 56 twin rooms.

LA GOMERA

Jardín Tecina Hotel (4 stars) €€€ *Lomada de Tecina, Playa de Santiago; Tel. (922) 14 58 50; fax 14 58 51.* A stylish complex set in its own extensive gardens on the cliffs. An ambiance of easy-going friendliness, combined with the peace and beauty of the surroundings, makes it a fantastic hideaway. Has an array of restaurants, bars, pools, numerous sports facilities and the hotel's own beach club. 434 rooms.

LA PALMA

Parador de la Palma (4 stars) €€ *El Zumacal, Breña Baja; Tel. (922) 43 58 28; fax 43 59 99.* A new parador located on the cliffs just to the south of, and overlooking, Santa Cruz. Traditionally Canarian in style and décor, with a delightful central patio, this has spacious rooms and pleasant gardens with a pool. 78 rooms.

LANZAROTE

Hotel Gran Meliá Salinas (5 stars) €€€/€€€€ *Avenida Islas Canarias s/n, Costa Teguise; Tel. (928) 59 00 40; fax 59 03 90; web site <www.solmelia.es>.* The island's largest and most luxurious hotel, and an integral part of the cultural heritage of Lanzarote. The stunning double atrium is filled with magnificent indoor gardens and waterfalls — the artistic creations, like the pool, of César Manrique. Over 300 rooms.

TENERIFE

Gran Hotel Bahia del Duque, Gran Meliá (5 stars GL) €€€€ *C/. Alcade Walter Paetzmann s/n, Costa Adeje; Tel. (922) 74 69 00; fax 74 69 25; web site <www.bahia-duque.com>.* An eclectic array of buildings set around a sub-tropical garden with pools, restaurants and bars that drop, over several levels, down to the beach. Traditionally dressed staff, peacocks roaming free and an amazing lobby will all impress. 362 rooms.

Hotel San Roque (3 stars) €€€ *C/. Esteban de Ponte 32, Garachico; Tel. (922) 13 34 35; fax 13 34 06; web site <www.hotel-sanroque.com>.* A beguiling and eclectic mix of a traditional 17th-century palace with traditional wooden beamed ceilings and balconies and modern art-deco. The rooms are well thought out, with CDs, satellite TV and even jacuzzi tubs. The pool is set in a charming patio. 20 rooms.

Recommended restaurants

Many restaurants offer cheaper fixed-price menus in addition to their *à-la-carte* selections; reservations are recommended for the more expensive places.

As a basic guide, we have used the following symbols to give some idea of the cost of dinner for two, excluding drinks.

€	below € 36.00
€€	€36.00–60 00
€€€	over € 60.00

ÁVILA

Doña Guismar €€ *Tomás Luís de Victoria 3; Tel. (920) 25 37 09.* Located in a beautifully restored building, this restaurant combines traditional style with classic and modern influences to create temptingly delicious dishes.

BARCELONA

Botafumeiro €€€ *Gran de Gràcia 81; Tel. (93) 218 42 30.* Diners are presented with perfectly prepared and presented fish and shellfish dishes that combine the best elements of Galician and Catalan cuisines. Botafumeiro is considered the best restaurant of its type in Barcelona. Closed Mondays, and Sunday evenings.

La Fonda Escudellers €€ *Carrer dels Escudellers 10; Tel. (93) 301 75 75.* This modern restaurant is set on two levels and is immensely popular, as the inevitable lines outside testify. It is worth the wait for very good food at very reasonable prices.

CÓRDOBA

El Churrasco €€/€€€ *Romero 16; Tel. (957) 29 08 17.* Charmingly located in a 14th-century house in the Jewish quarter, El

Churrasco has various dining areas each uniquely decorated. The seasonal cuisine is based on natural products with wines from its own Museo del Vino (Wine Museum). Closed August.

COSTA DEL SOL

Taberna del Alabardero €€€ *Muelle Benabola s/n, Puerto Banús; Tel. (95) 281 27 94.* On the Main Quay overlooking the luxurious yachts that crowd Puerto Banús, this is one of southern Spain's most prestigious and elegant restaurants. The menu features Mediterranean and Basque specialties as well as international selections, and there is a wide-ranging wine list. Open daily for lunch and dinner.

GRANADA

Sevilla €€ *Oficios 12; Tel. (958) 22 12 23.* Granada's most famous restaurant was also once a favorite of García Lorca, the poet and dramatist. The menu offers a good mixture of local Granadino and Andalucían specialties. Closed Sunday evening.

MADRID

Lhardy €€€ *San Jerónimo 8; Tel. (91) 522 22 07.* At first glance this looks like a very elegant and old-fashioned delicatessen store. Founded in 1839, that is exactly what it is downstairs, but head upstairs and you will find a suite of elegant dining rooms, where you can expect a traditional gastronomic treat, whatever you decide to select from the menu.

Casa Santa Cruz €€/€€€ *La Bolsa 12; Tel. (91) 521 86 23.* This is probably the most beautiful and unusual restaurant in Madrid. The building dates from the 15th century, and was once a chapel of the Santa Cruz church, later serving as the first stock exchange. The menu features dishes from traditional Castilian recipes.

Spain

Taberna del Alabardero €€€ *Felipe V 6; Tel. (91) 247 25 77.* Located close to the Royal Palace, this was originally called the Guardia de Alabarderos tavern, because it was a popular watering hole for the guards who used to march by on duty and later return for a drink. The owner, Luis de Lezama, a former priest and delightfully charming host, has fashioned a wonderful restaurant here that has sister restaurants, all of the same name, in Puerto Banús and Sevilla in Spain, and in Washington DC in the US. The food is Basque and remarkably good value -- especially the *menú del día*.

PAMPLONA

Josetzo €€€ *Plaza Príncipe de Viana 1; Tel. (948) 22 20 97.* Widely regarded as the city's finest restaurant, the specialties at Josetzo include fresh fish dishes and frozen dessert truffles. Closed Sunday (except during San Fermín) and August.

SAN SEBASTIÁN

Arzak €€€ *Alto de Miracruz 21; Tel. (943) 27 84 65.* This Michelin three-star restaurant specialises in traditional Basque cuisine. The superbly prepared game and seafood dishes are served with the attention and precision that you would expect from the Michelin stars, and accompanied by classic wines. Closed Sunday evening, Monday, and two weeks in June and November.

SANTIAGO DE COMPOSTELA

Restaurante A Barrola €€ *Rua Franco 29; Tel. (981) 57 79 99.* Passers-by are tempted in by a window display consisting of a sumptuous array of fish and shellfish. The house specialty is a shellfish combination, designed to be shared by two. If you cannot find someone to share with, try the octopus in garlic with tiny mussels, which is equally delicious.

SEGOVIA

José María €€ *Cronista Lecea 11; Tel. (921) 46 11 11.* A firm favorite in Segovia, José María serves traditional Castilian fare with fine local wines in a lively, rustic ambiance. It is hard not to be tempted to over-indulge by the wide selection of delicious *tapas* on show in the bar.

SALAMANCA

Restaurante Chapeau €€€ *España 20; Tel. (923) 21 17 26.* Considered one of the best restaurants in Salamanca, the Chapeau has a traditional ambiance. Dishes on the *La Creatividad* menu can be ordered as whole plates or in smaller portions that can be combined to form a *Degustación* menu. Another menu specializes in local regional dishes.

SEVILLA

Egaña Oriza €€€ *C/. San Fernando 41; Tel. (95) 442 72 1.* This renowned restauranta enjoys a privileged location in a beautiful building just across from Sevilla's old Tobacco Factory (the setting for Bizet's opera *Carmen*). The Egaña Oriza is famous for Jose María Egaña's dishes, which combine Basque influences with Andalucían traditions. The wine list features Spanish and international vintages. Closed Saturday lunchtime, Sunday and August.

Restaurante Marea Grande €€ *C/. Diego Angulo Inigiuez 16; Tel. and fax (95) 453 80 00.* Just outside the city center, this has a delightful ambiance and décor and offers an amazing array of seafood and shellfish, with a fine wine list and excellent service.

TOLEDO

Casón de los López de Toledo €€€ *Sillería 3; Tel. (925) 25 47 74; fax 25 72 82.* Located in an impressive historic building just off the Plaza de Zocodover, the dining rooms are full of antiques and works of art. These complement the traditional cuisine, which is often embellished by modern touches. The wine list is one of the most informative of its kind.

VALENCIA

Rías Gallegas €€€ *Cirilo Amoros 4; Tel. (96) 351 21 25.* Established for over 30 years, this restaurant specializes in Galician cuisine. Unusually, many of the dishes can be ordered in half portions. Closed Sunday and last three weeks in August.

THE BALEARIC ISLANDS

IBIZA

Sueno de Estrellas €€€/€€€€ *Miguel; Tel. (971) 33 45 00.* The delightful gourmet restaurant of the Hacienda hotel is set on two levels overlooking the pool and cliffs. Whether you select the daily menu, the special 7-course menu or *à la carte,* expect delightfully thought-out and well-presented dishes.

Restaurante del Carmen € *Platja Cala D'Hort; Tel. (971) 80 00 95.* What this lacks in *haute-cuisine* and style it more than makes up for in other things. It overlooks the quiet beach and has, arguably, the best views of the mystic Es Vedra rock on the island.

MALLORCA

Tristan €€€€ *Puerto Portals; Tel. (971) 67 55 47.* Tristan is the only Michelin two-star restaurant in the Balearics and represents the pinnacle of cuisine on Mallorca. It has a wonderful location over-looking the large yachts in the marina, modern art on the walls and attentive, but not obsequious, service. Wonderfully delicate and esoterically presented examples of international cuisine are created by Gerhard Schwaiger. Closed Monday — except mid-June to mid-

September — mid-November to mid-December, and the last three weeks in January.

Koldo Royo €€€/€€€€ *Ingeniero Gabriel Roca 3; Tel. (971)73 24 35.* On the Paseo Maritimo, overlooking the harbor, this is a very fine restaurant indeed. Koldo Royo trained in San Sebastian, and that shows in his imaginative Basque recipes. Expect delightfully presented dishes such as "warm and cold cream of green peas and asparagus soup," which is drunk from a glass. Closed Sunday night.

El Pi €€€/€€€€ *Formentor; Tel. (971) 89 91 00.* This is the gourmet restaurant of the Hotel Formentor. With the pool and Mediterranean as a backdrop, enjoy classical Mallorcan and international-style cuisine. The six-course *degustation menu* is a particular delight.

La Reserva Rotana €€€/€€€€ *Manacor-Mallorca: Tel. (971) 84 56 85.* No need to leave if you are staying here, and well worth coming to if you are staying at a nearby resort. The antique-furnished dining room has a high, wood-beamed ceiling; choose the three- or four-course — or if you have room, the extravagant six-course — *menu dégustacion.*

MINORCA

Es Plá €€/€€€ *Pasaje Es Plá, Fornells; Tel. (971) 37 66 55.* The island's most famous restaurant, patronized by King Juan Carlos, who comes here for the *caldereta de langousta,* a delicious lobster stew. If your wallet will not accommodate the royal favorite, there are plenty of other good things to try.

THE CANARY ISLANDS

GRAN CANARIA

Restaurante Gurufer €€€ *C/. León y Castilla 274, 35005 Las Palmas; Tel. (928) 24 40 07.* Set in one of the most distinguished old houses in town, this has a very classical ambiance, and the cuisine to match. The very tasteful menu specializes in old-fashioned Canarian dishes, with fine wines to match.

LA GOMERA

Restaurante El Laurel €€€€ *Lomada de Tecina, 38810 Playa de Santiago; Tel. (922) 14 58 50.* The *à la carte* restaurant of the Jardín Tecina resort is located by the beach, and reached by means of an elevator that passes through the cliff. The fantastic location is combined with a romantic ambiance, live guitar music, *haute cuisine* and fine wines — a perfect choice for a romantic night out.

LA PALMA

Restaurante La Placeta €€€ *Borrero, 1; Tel. (922) 41 52 73.* Located in a charming old house, this has a delightful ambiance. Wooden floors, beams, staircase and old windows complement home-cooked international-style cuisine with an emphasis on fish, meats and sauces. Open daily from 7pm to 11pm.

LANZAROTE

La Era €€€ *Yaiza; Tel. (928) 83 00 16.* Set in a charming 300-year-old typical Canarian country house, with a whitewashed patio courtyard decked with flowers, La Era serves outstanding island specialties. There is also an art-filled wood-beamed bar that serves snacks and light meals, and a craft shop. The décor owes much to César Manrique's artistic creations.

TENERIFE

Mi Vaca Y Yo €€/€€€ *Cruz Verde 3, Puerto de la Cruz; Tel. (922) 38 52 47.* Superb international food is served here in an exotic subtropical setting. A favorite tourist haunt, this restaurant is good value and serves fresh grilled fish and seafood.

INDEX